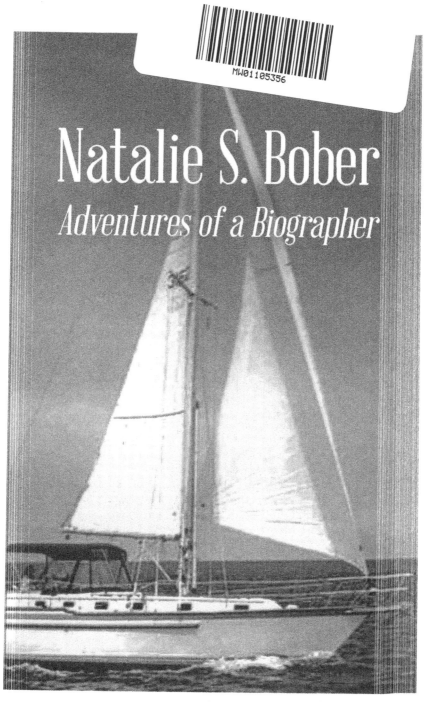

Natalie S. Bober

Adventures of a Biographer

outskirts
press

Books By Natalie S. Bober

William Wordsworth: The Wandering Poet
A Restless Spirit: The Story of Robert Frost
Louise Nevelson: Breaking Tradition
Let's Pretend: Poems of Flight and Fancy
Thomas Jefferson: Man on A Mountain
Marc Chagall: Painter of Dreams
A Restless Spirit: The Story of Robert Frost
(an enriched edition)
Abigail Adams: Witness to A Revolution
Countdown to Independence
Thomas Jefferson: Draftsman of A Nation
Papa Is A Poet: A Story About Robert Frost

For all the BEGs - passed and present

With much love

Table of Contents

Acknowledgements

Over these many years, as I have researched and written eleven books, I have developed friendships as well as debts of gratitude to many people. All have been acknowledged in the specific books, and are too numerous to specify again here. Many people, however, have been particularly helpful with *Adventures of A Biographer.* My granddaughter Jody Hoffman read it in its very early stages, encouraged me to continue, and helped me organize my thoughts. My children Stephen Bober and Betsy Bober Polivy, and my granddaughter Joelle Polivy Schatz have helped it take shape through many revisions. They read the manuscript with meticulous attention to detail and asked the kind of questions every writer cherishes.

My son Marc Bober inspired me to make sailing another big adventure.

My grandson, Evan Polivy, brought me untold joy with his beautiful design of the cover.

My young friend Nate Schatz appraised the manuscript with a critical eye from his unique perspective, all the while pointing out both the good and the bad in his written commentary.

Treasured friends Marcia Marshal, Sylvie Heyman, and Rhoda Fishkin offered encouragement and advice, and made many fine suggestions, as did Sophie Netenal. And Rhoda Fishkin became for me a lee port in a storm.

I am most grateful to all of them.

My husband, Larry Bober, has for many years borne the burden of living with a wife who was living in the eighteenth and nineteenth centuries – not an easy task! But he has done so with grace, willingly undertaking any twentieth or twenty-first century task that would allow me the freedom to write. His careful reading of all my manuscripts, and his probing questions, have been invaluable. Accompanying me on numerous research trips, all the while taking his extraordinary photographs, has doubled the joy. His patience, his understanding, and his love make it all possible.

In fact, it strikes me that, over the years, my research and writing have served as a bond that has brought our family – and our extended family - even closer together. It is a joy that has helped me keep a legacy alive.

$\mathcal{P}$reface

Many years ago, early on the morning of a cold, but sunny day in March, a very shy and timid fifteen-year-old high school junior took the New York City subway to 116th Street and, with great trepidation, walked into the fabled halls of Columbia University. As editor of the Hunter College High School newspaper, called "What's What," she had been invited by the Columbia Scholastic Press Association to accept its first place award for excellence.

I was that girl!

Can you imagine the thrill it is for me today to have been able to write this book? If only we could see into the future when we were young, and know where our efforts would take us!

Certainly, when I graduated from Hunter College five years later, I had no sense at all of where I would be today. What I did know was that books would always be a thread that was tightly woven into the fabric of my life. That began with my first summer job – at age sixteen – just after I had graduated from high school – working in the stacks at the main branch of the New York Public Library.

Little did I know then that I would one day be writing books that would have a special niche on those shelves.

1

An Incredible Journey

"Writing lives is the devil!" the author Virginia Woolf once wrote to her sister Vanessa. For me, the reverse has always been true. Since I stumbled into the role of biographer quite by accident, writing lives – and the research it entails – has been an exciting adventure.

As I read, interview, travel, or study the work my subjects produced – whether it be paintings or poetry, personal letters, or the Declaration of Independence – trying to build bridges into their minds and their hearts – to see and hear and feel what they did, I never know where my research will lead me. As I try to catch the essence of the lives I'm investigating, I must study the past with a revealing searchlight, all the while looking for details. Like a hog digging for truffles, I'm always after those dark, hidden morsels.

I must learn about the people who influenced my subject – family, teachers, friends, the day by day events taking place, the clothing, the food, the art of the times – all the while trying to capture the sights, the sounds, even the smells of a place. Just as time and place are at the heart of much good fiction, so they are essential in a good biography. In order to present history I must possess the period myself. I must understand it thoroughly.

For a writer to breathe life into people who lived a long time ago, she must eavesdrop across the centuries to find the details that give the past a pulse, and that help you, the reader, see it and understand it. It's the search for these small details that is often the most interesting and exciting part of the process for me. I feel like a detective searching for clues. The excitement comes from search and discovery, from recreating a life from details and making a story out of the chaos of reality. This is the challenge of biography that has kept me on a perpetual treasure hunt.

Many years ago, in a series of lectures at Cambridge University, André Maurois, the French biographer and novelist best known for his biographies that maintain the narrative interest of novels, spoke of the fascinating relationship between a biographer and a portrait painter. That analogy has always intrigued me. Maurois asked, "Isn't it curious how the metaphor of the portrait painter crops up as soon as one begins to talk of the biographer?"

This metaphor was brought home to me personally when I took a course some years ago entitled "High Art in the Low Countries." Standing in front of paintings of the masters in the great museums of Belgium and Holland, I found myself taking notes on the relationship of the portraits to biography.

Indeed, I like to think of myself as a portrait painter, but a painter whose palette is words. Most lives are mosaics, accumulations of little bits of reality, shaped into an image. The biographer is the artist, under oath, shaping this mosaic. The painter recreates on canvas the visual appearance of a life and a personality. The eye of a fine biographer, like that of a portrait painter, captures that special gleam of character that makes the reader feel the presence of a recognizable, approachable life – a real person. She portrays the human being behind the great artist or statesman, and sets her subject against the canvas of history.

In order to give texture to a life, the biographer must lift the curtain of time and describe the milieu from which her subjects sprang. She eavesdrops across the centuries, so to speak, looking for clues.

The story becomes, then, not simply the life of a subject, but the portrait of an era as well. And - in this way biography becomes a prism of history. In fact, biography has been described as the human heart of history. The biographer, then, becomes a historian as well as a portrait painter.

But the biographer must be a storyteller as well – a storyteller whose facts are true. Research and documentation must be thorough and meticulous. Careful reference notes, full bibliography, illustrations – all must be included. I must be certain that the details – the facts – I use are accurate.

While I may not invent my facts as a novelist does, I may invent my form, and in that sense, the biographer becomes a creative artist. I must select and arrange the details I've gathered in my research into a story that draws readers in and keeps them turning the pages as though they were reading a fine novel. To capture and hold the interest of an audience has been the aim of every storyteller since the beginning of time.

As I write, I have to be careful that the biography I'm writing doesn't become just a dull list of facts. The personality of the hero must shine through. This is where the art comes in. Telling a story requires arrangement, composition, planning – just like a painting. Good writing not only conveys information, it has balance, form, and grace. It becomes a work of art. There should be no need to choose between accuracy and beauty.

In writing, I am constantly bewitched by the rhythm and sound of the words, and by the interaction of their sound and sense. I always read my work out loud. It is only when we read our writing aloud that we can tell if it's alive.

And as I write the life of a *creative* artist – a poet, a painter, a sculptor – I must illumine, in some small measure, the mystery and magical process of creation. Here, too, a sense of time and place is essential.

How did William Wordsworth or Robert Frost come to write that poem? Why did Marc Chagall paint a fiddler on the roof, or lovers floating over the rooftops? Why did Louise Nevelson make big black wooden boxes? How do Abigail Adams's letters allow us, today, to be witness to a revolution?

4

Over the years, in my quest for answers to these and other such questions, I have had many extraordinary experiences that have enriched my life and provided me with clues that helped to unlock secrets of the inner person I was struggling to understand.

As I look back on those years and reflect on the way in which my role as a biographer has slowly and subtly evolved, I realize that my seemingly quiet life has had its full share of exciting interludes – little dramas that have fallen into the course of an otherwise ordinary day – happenings that never found their way into the books I was writing, but nonetheless provided the joy I experienced in doing the necessary research. It is these stories – often serendipitous, sometimes funny, sometimes moving, always fascinating – that I would like to share with you, my readers.

I sometimes have the feeling that every biography I have written is a part of my autobiography. Remembered experiences and emotions grant me a lens of empathy through which I can view my subject. One's writing and one's personal life frequently mesh. We are the stories we tell.

"The work you do…is your reflection," the artist Louise Nevelson once told me. "Who is an artist?" she asked. "No one gives us that title. We make our lives," she continued. Indeed, I have been struck by the way in which each life that I have investigated has in some way changed me, and helped me to gain perspective on my own life.

I invite you now to journey back in time with me, to peek behind closed doors and help me re-live some of my adventures and to speak again to the fascinating people I have met along the way. I will attempt to make it possible for you to experience, albeit vicariously through the stories I tell you, some of the joy and excitement of my odyssey.

As you join me on my treasure hunt for these details, some of which often became the details of my life as well, we will meet not only the people whose lives I have documented, people whose achievements can serve as an inspiration to all who read about them, but those wonderful present-day people who have helped me immeasurably in my attempts to record six remarkable lives.

2

William Wordsworth: The Wandering Poet

My career as a biographer began when I was awakened one night with a burning pain in my leg. I knew immediately that this was not simply a leg cramp that would disappear in a little while.

The problem, which involved extensive testing to determine what was causing the pain,[1] kept me off my feet for six months. During that time, I chanced upon an article in *Writer Magazine* about writing biographies for young people. My husband challenged me to try. "You've always wanted to write," he said. "Besides, it will keep you sane." Never one to ignore a challenge, I decided to take him up on it. I *had* always wanted to write, but I'd never had the nerve to try. I didn't think my writing was good enough. Until then, I had been raising

---

1   It was ultimately diagnosed as peripheral neuritis, a painful nerve condition.

three children while working as a reading consultant and diagnostician.

So, lying in bed and contemplating my husband's suggestion about writing biography, I began to think about the English poet William Wordsworth and how much I loved his poetry. Coincidentally, my husband and I had recently taken a trip to London and on up to the Lake District in the northwest of England, where Wordsworth had lived. It was our first trip abroad. I had been an English major in college, and had studied the Romantic poets Percy Bysshe Shelley, John Keats, and William Wordsworth, among others. In fact, my senior thesis in college had been on this subject.

I began to think, too, about the love of England that I had absorbed from my English grandmother, who had lived with us all the while that I was growing up, and whom I adored. Every day when I came home from school, it was my grandmother who was waiting for me with freshly baked cookies, strong English tea, and wonderful tales of England. I never tired of listening to them. To this day the memory of her remains a constant source of inspiration.

Continuing to consider the possibility of writing a biography brought back memories of the musty smell of the old books on Charing Cross Road, the book center of London, where my husband and I had walked, searching out – and finding – treasures, particularly a leather bound edition of *The Poetical Works of William Wordsworth*, published in 1913.

For years I had yearned to see the places

that had inspired Wordsworth to write "Daffodils," "The Rainbow," "Tintern Abbey," "Composed upon Westminster Bridge," and his great autobiographical poem, "Prelude." I had dreamed of seeing the area where the daffodils bloomed that his sister Dorothy had described so vividly, and that had been such an influence on him.

I recalled our drive from the town of Chester, a medieval city enclosed in its original walls, toward "Wordsworth country" (in the Lake District). The narrow, winding road bordered by stone walls seemed to outline the surrounding mountains. It was raining – not unusual in England – but just as we approached Hawkshead, the sixteenth century village where the young William Wordsworth had gone to school, the rain stopped, the sun came out, and a rainbow appeared in the sky. Instantly, and in unison, we recited aloud Wordsworth's poem: "My heart leaps up when I behold/A rainbow in the sky." It was so perfect it almost seemed contrived.

We visited the little schoolhouse where William had carved his initials into a desk. In the nearby town of Grasmere, we explored Dove Cottage, where he had lived with his sister Dorothy and later with his wife Mary and their children. We saw the original manuscripts of some of his poems.

As we wandered through his house we could see how it illustrated his belief in "plain living, high thinking, no pretense." The cottage held an oak dining table, a two hundred and fifty year old grandfather clock with its beautiful carving, and the couch on which he rested and reflected on scenes he had witnessed. He referred to the couch specifically in the last stanza of his poem "Daffodils":

> For oft, when on my couch I lie,
> In vacant or in pensive mood,
> They flash upon that inward eye
> Which is the bliss of solitude;
> And then my heart with pleasure fills,
> And dances with the daffodils.

Dove Cottage helped me to visualize what life must have been like in Grasmere in the nineteenth century.

We had a traditional "high tea" at the Old England Hotel, overlooking Lake Windermere.

Later we drove to southeastern Wales. Along the banks of the Wye River, we beheld the breathtaking ruins of Tintern Abbey, a medieval monastery with its walls and arches rising from a narrow valley floor, and surrounded by a landscape of wild natural beauty. It was in the valley of the Wye River that Wordsworth had first begun to hope that he might someday produce an "enduring and creative" work of poetry about nature. It was his second visit to the Wye five years later, in 1798, that prompted the beautiful "Lines Composed A Few Miles Above Tintern Abbey," shortly after he, his sister Dorothy, and their friend Samuel Taylor Coleridge had walked there.

"Tintern Abbey" is Wordsworth's prayer of thanksgiving for his ability to see, enjoy, and retain a landscape, as well as a description of the changes in his feelings over the preceding five years:

> *...I have learned*
> *To look on nature, not as in the hour*
> *Of thoughtless youth; but hearing oftentimes*
> *The still, sad music of humanity*

I knew from past reading that Wordsworth had been a rebel, but a rebel and a gentleman at the same time. William Wordsworth would be my perfect subject.

And so the research began. Still unable to walk, I prevailed upon my mother and my dear friend Lea Green to bring me books from the library. They brought biographies of William Wordsworth. They brought biographies of other poets writing at that time – particularly Wordsworth's friend Samuel Taylor Coleridge. They brought books about Georgian England and about the history of the time in which Wordsworth lived. They brought books of analysis and critiques of his poetry. I wrote to publishing houses to order still more books: about the age of English Romanticism; the French Revolution that was taking place at that time; Georgian London; the letters of Dorothy and William Wordsworth; and life in Grasmere, to mention just some.

I re-read the poetry of William Wordsworth.

At one point, I counted thirty-two books surrounding me on the bed. To be a writer, I was discovering, one must first be a reader! Soon I decided that I had better begin to put some thoughts on paper. As I organized my notes and tentatively began to write, the pain in my leg seemed to be subsiding.

When I was finally able to walk a bit, my husband all but drove me up the steps of the library so I could do some looking on my own.

Eventually I had a sense of how I wanted to structure the book. I would show how Wordsworth's poems were an outgrowth of the life he lived, and how the era in which he was living influenced him. I would portray his childhood, the loss of his mother when he was only seven years old, his school years, his relationship with his brothers and, particularly, the special relationship he had with his sister Dorothy. And I would describe how, at the age of twenty, instead of studying for his upcoming exams at Cambridge University, with a friend he tramped 2,000 miles through revolutionary France, walked the Alpine tracks of Switzerland, and the river valleys of Germany and Belgium, so that years later he could write:

> *Bliss was it in that dawn to be alive*
> *But to be young was very heaven!*

I started to write in earnest. Soon I sent a query letter, then a proposal, an outline, and sample chapters to editors at publishing houses, all of whom responded: "No, thank you." Most told me, kindly, that the book was a great idea, the chapters that I had sent were well written, but a book about William Wordsworth would not sell. Young people today just don't read his poetry, they said.

Devastated, but determined, I continued to send it around – one publishing house at a time. Twenty-one editors returned it. The twenty-second editor who read the manuscript was Gloria Mosesson at Thomas Nelson Publishers. Gloria was an Anglophile – she loved all things English – and she was willing to take a chance. But she wanted a complete manuscript before she would give me a contract, **and** she wanted a new beginning. Her advice that an opening paragraph must grab a reader's attention has stood me in good stead. I have learned that first lines can provide a window into the entire work – for the writer as well as for the reader. They set the tone for the entire piece. I was happy to comply.

Just after I learned that a publisher was, indeed, interested in publishing my book, I learned of a writing course being given at Hofstra University and decided to enroll. It was a good decision. The course was being taught by L.J. Davis, a tall, thin man with a wry wit, an obvious love of writing, and a strong desire to communicate that love – and the necessary skills – to his students.

When I asked him if he would read the beginning of the book I was attempting to write – my first attempt – he readily agreed, then volunteered to come to my apartment and critique it for me.

As I waited for him to arrive at the appointed time, I wondered what the concierge at our staid little apartment building would think when a very tall young man, wearing his trademark cowboy boots and ten gallon hat, arrived and asked to be sent up to my apartment in the middle of the day. Who would she think he was? She never commented.

His visit – and his suggestions – truly set me on my way. His major piece of advice was to slow down in my writing and include more detail. This has become for me one of the basic rules of writing biography. The first page of *William Wordsworth: The Wandering Poet* is perhaps the best illustration of this: Thinking back to our visit to William's childhood home in Cockermouth, England, I remembered and could describe the four-poster bed where William's young and beautiful mother lay ominously still and pale, the heavy velvet draperies at the window giving the room a somber look, the flickering candle on the candle stand providing the only light, and the highboy that loomed tall and menacing to the small boy. All these details create an aura of impending sadness. My editor approved.

When the book was finally published, after four years of research and writing, *William Wordsworth: The Wandering Poet* was named by the Child Study Association to its list: "Best Biographies of the Year," and I was off and running – literally and figuratively. In the interim, my leg pain had gradually disappeared. I was, in the words of writer Mary Catherine Bateson, "composing a life," my own as well as those of the six extraordinary people whose lives I would eventually document. I was becoming a biographer. It was only then that I remembered what my classmates had said of me in my Hunter College High School Yearbook:

> She has literary talent
> And successful she will be
> If the critics like her books
> As much as we like Natalie.

After I finished the Wordsworth book, I flew to England to visit my daughter, Betsy, who was studying at an international program based at Oxford University. A letter from her had precipitated the trip. It's one that I have saved these many years, and treasure still. It points up the far-reaching influence my writing has had on my family. It begins: "I think it began many years ago when you became an author, but Wordsworth's life in the Bober household did not end with your book. Willie and I are great friends. I have never been as excited about anything academic as I am now. I only wish you were here to share it with me."

And share we did. On that trip Betsy introduced me to Jonathan Wordsworth, her professor for a course on the poetry of William Wordsworth that she was taking at Oxford. Jonathan Wordsworth (1932-2006) was the poet's great-great-grand nephew, the great-great grandson of his youngest brother, Christopher.

As I sat in his class with her, listening to William Wordsworth's poems being analyzed by his great-great-grand nephew, I couldn't help wondering who would ever have thought, when I was an eighteen-year-old student in Dr. Ryan's Romantic Poetry class at Hunter College, that one day I would be here at Oxford University with my daughter and with a member of William Wordsworth's family!

Later, at Professor Wordsworth's invitation, we visited his "rooms" in Exeter College, Oxford, at the top of a narrow, winding staircase. There we shared some hot soup and sherry with him and talked about his illustrious ancestor. That visit remains one of my most unforgettable experiences.

After meeting with Professor Wordsworth, Betsy and I drove to Dove Cottage in Grasmere. There we saw my biography, *William Wordsworth: The Wandering Poet*, displayed in the window of the little Dove Cottage gift shop, an image that has remained in my mind's eye these many years.

NSB outside Dove Cottage window
Photo courtesy of Betsy Bober Polivy

3

Robert Frost:
A Restless Spirit

I came to the English poet William Wordsworth through my love of his poetry, so it was natural that I would choose the American poet Robert Frost as my next subject. Frost's life-long love affair with the craft of writing is the quality about him that speaks most eloquently to me. Both men wrote in "language really used by men" and both call across the years to me as kindred restless spirits.

When I first approached my research on Robert Frost, I decided that the best place to begin would be close to home. I had learned that the Bobst Library at New York University, in its Fales Library/Special Collections, owned all the books Frost had collected in his lifetime – and many more. In 1964, the year after her father had died, Frost's daughter Lesley presented to the library the complete collection of the nearly two thousand books in his personal library. Included in this treasure trove were newspaper articles and books containing Robert Frost's own marginalia, his comments on what he was reading.

In the Fales Library, on the strength of a letter from my editor, Marcia Marshall, attesting to the fact that I was a scholar researching the life of Robert Frost, I was given permission to browse the collection, and a desk where I could leave my work at the end of the day and begin again the next morning. At that early stage in my research it was a heady experience.

Later, I made trips to the Amherst College Library and the Jones Library in Amherst, Massachusetts. I had learned of the wealth of material held in these libraries from the bibliographies and the reference notes in the books I had already read. At the Jones Library I was permitted to see (and my husband to photograph) such treasures as Frost's original manuscript of "The Runaway" – with the whimsical sketch of a young colt who had run away at the top of the page. The boys whom Frost was teaching at Amherst had asked him for a poem for the June 1918 issue of the *Amherst Monthly.* Frost gave them *The Runaway.* The boys knew that Frost had written the poem for them and they understood that the little colt in the poem was really the runaway in the poet and in themselves. Frost had run away from Harvard and from Dartmouth.

I visited Dartmouth College in New Hampshire specifically to interview Edward Lathem, Dean of Libraries at the college. He had been a very good friend of Frost later in the poet's life, and could have given me much more information than he did. That was my fault. I had not done my homework. I had not read enough before I went to Dartmouth to know about Lathem's close relationship with Frost, so did not know all the questions to ask. That experience taught me to seek out specific books – and people – by what I found in the bibliography and/or the acknowledgements of what I considered a fine book about my subject. I never made that mistake again. Over the years I learned to prepare appropriate questions that would engage my interviewee in a conversation that would help me to garner important information.

I loved, also, to peruse the shelves of old and out of print bookstores. One never knows what treasures might be lurking there!

In Lawrence, Massachusetts, where Frost went to high school, Eartha Dengler, founder and executive director of Immigrant City Archives, did considerable sleuthing for me in order to locate photographs and information on that city at the end of the nineteenth century.

A tiny newspaper article in the *New York Times* announcing a celebration of the life of Robert Frost, led my husband and me to make a car trip to Ripton, Vermont. The celebration would take place at the three-room log cabin where Frost had lived alone for the last twenty-five years of his life, after his wife, Elinor, had died. I had no idea what or whom I would find there, but decided I had to go. I would be able to see the inside of the cabin, and to meet some of the people who had known Frost and had played a significant role in his life. Perhaps one of them might offer up some interesting and worthwhile information. I might gain some insight into Frost's life at that time. So we headed to Ripton and the Homer Noble Farm on which the cabin is situated.

Arriving in Ripton on the day before the celebration, we decided to find our way to the farm we would be visiting the next day. As we approached, we saw a woman hanging wash to dry in the sunshine. We guessed that she might be Kathleen Morrison. She had been a dear friend of Frost, and she lived on the farm. My husband suggested that I introduce myself to her. Hesitantly, and after much urging from him, I gathered my courage, got out of the car, and approached her.

The lady was, indeed, Kathleen Morrison, who was most gracious and warm in her welcome to us. Knowing her did make the following day far easier to navigate. When we arrived in the morning, Mrs. Morrison immediately introduced us to a host of people, including Alfred Edwards, President of Holt, Rinehart, and Winston (Robert Frost's publisher). Edwards was also executor of the Robert Frost Estate. He invited us to have lunch with him and his wife, Eleanor, on the terrace of his home nearby. The house was situated high on a hill

with a breathtaking view of the Green Mountains surrounding us. He told us that these were the hills where
he had walked with Robert Frost. Ultimately, as my
work progressed on the Frost book, and my research
deepened, Al Edwards came to be most helpful to me.

Every biography that I write offers me an excuse
to travel. Documents can never tell the whole story. I
must go to the territory. I must walk where my subjects
walked, and see what they must have seen. The language of landscape is essential.

For *A Restless Spirit: The Story of Robert Frost*, in
addition to visiting Frost's several homes in Vermont and
New Hampshire, we climbed the hills of San Francisco
to explore the city where Robert Frost was born. We
saw the view that the young Rob Frost must have
seen of the schooners sailing into San Francisco Bay.
We visited the mill town of Lawrence, Massachusetts,
where Frost lived and attended high school after his
father died. We wandered through the Derry Farm in
New Hampshire where so much of Frost's poetry was
born. In the farmhouse we saw the beds that his children could choose among to sleep in each night. There
were no assigned beds and no assigned bedtimes. The
children just drifted off to bed one by one as they got
sleepy while their parents read to them.

We photographed the stone walls that inspired his
famous poem "Mending Wall." We photographed Hyla
Brook, the little brook that meanders through the Derry
Farm and was the inspiration for the poem "Hyla Brook."
And, inside the cabin at Ripton, we photographed the

famous Morris chair in which Frost sat to "make" his poems. That photo hangs on a wall in our home. The chair, sitting majestically near the fireplace, made it possible for me to picture Frost sitting in it, in the warmth of the fire, deep in thought, and writing.

When we visited B J Dennis, a friend who lived in San Francisco, and mentioned to him that I had just begun to research the life of Robert Frost, our friend exclaimed, "I know his granddaughter!" He immediately telephoned her, and she invited us to visit the next morning. Over a cup of coffee Robin Hudnut consented to write an introduction to my book, **if** it spoke to her.

Over the next few years, as I continued my research and writing, Robin and I corresponded. I had learned that she was an artist but that she was not painting because of the demands of raising five young children. From three thousand miles across the country, I continually urged her to try. After all, I was raising three children, teaching, and writing. She must try, I told her. Her grandfather would want her to use her talent.

Early in 1980, my husband had to be in San Francisco on business. I had a finished Frost manuscript, so I went to California with him. When we arrived, I telephoned Robin to ask her to read the manuscript, and to invite her to join us for dinner one evening. She agreed, but then said that we must come to her home first. She had something to show us.

As we entered her living room on the appointed evening, there, in front of us, still damp on its easel, was a painting of the tiny bent figure of her grandfather, wending his way up the snow covered hillside towards his cabin in Ripton. Robin had heeded my advice and had begun to paint again. This was the result of her first effort.

"Oh," I said immediately, with tears welling up in my eyes, "what a book jacket that would make!" We photographed the painting and brought the photos back to New York with us to show to Marcia Marshall, my editor at Atheneum Publishers. She responded immediately, "Oh, what a book jacket that would make!"

Robin was pleased with my story of her grandfather's life, and wrote a moving introduction. Her beautiful jacket helped *A Restless Spirit: The Story of Robert Frost* to "walk" off the shelves of bookstores and libraries.

Robin Hudnut's Book Jacket

Some years later, when the book was about to go out of print, an editor at Henry Holt & Co. phoned and invited me to write a new enlarged and enriched edition of *A Restless Spirit* that they would publish. It would contain many more poems and photographs than the original, as well as a new book jacket.

Thus, I made my second trip to Dartmouth, knowing that I would find there a plethora of photographs of all things related to Robert Frost. Indeed, Philip Cronenwett, chief of special collections,

23

made the entire Frost collection available to me. What an exciting adventure it became for me to look through hundreds of photographs, choosing freely among them for inclusion in what would eventually become a new edition of *A Restless Spirit*.

It was then that Robin shared more memories of her grandfather, as well as a treasure trove of family photographs. She also found for me the perfect picture of San Francisco in the late nineteenth century, just as Frost, as a young boy, would have seen it.

Robin and I continue to correspond, to share each other's joys and sorrows, and to visit whenever we can. In 2008, when *A Restless Spirit* was chosen "Book of the Year" by the Vermont Humanities Council, Robin came east to share the celebration with me.

As I think about Robin, and about my biography of her grandfather, I remember the period when I was attempting to write the chapter in the book about the birth of Robin, which resulted in the death of Marjorie, Frost's daughter and Robin's mother. During my researching and writing, I had learned much about Marjorie, and had come to love her. A bright-eyed and alert child, and a free spirit in whose poetry her father saw much promise, Marjorie loved to curl up with a book in front of the fire in the farmhouse while the snow swirled outside. In one of her poems she described herself:

> *For she has lived on mountain air*
> *And stayed a little child.*

Now the chapter I was writing simply wouldn't come together. I struggled over this one piece for three weeks, all the while feeling slightly ill. Finally, the reason came to me. Because I loved the Marjorie of my research and my imagination, I simply could not let her die. It was only when I came to understand what was happening, that sheer will power helped me to put my thoughts on paper.

While I was still researching my book, I travelled to other houses in Vermont and New Hampshire where Frost had lived. One is in Franconia, New Hampshire, where I saw a piano that I will long remember:

Memories are often triggered by an inanimate object. For me a piano conjures up memories of my mother, and of the marriage of Elinor and Robert Frost, and both are bound inextricably into *A Restless Spirit: The Story of Robert Frost*. My mother struggled to be able to buy a Baldwin spinet as a gift for my fifteenth birthday. Robert Frost bought a piano on impulse for Elinor, knowing full well that it was an extravagance he could ill afford. It still sits in the old farmhouse in Franconia. Today, mine sits in a house in Aberdeen, South Dakota, where some of my great grandchildren are learning to play it.

My mother had been the managing editor of *The Reader's Guide to Periodical Literature*[2]. Later, when I was a young student, she had patiently taught me how

---

2   Considered the index that revolutionized the world of research, it is a reference guide to published articles in magazines and scholarly journals, organized by article subject.

to do careful research. It was she who read my first two manuscripts, edited them with meticulous attention to detail, and indexed them before she died. In fact, she suffered the cerebral hemorrhage that led to her death as she sat at her dining room table, index cards and manuscript pages spread out around her, preparing the index for *A Restless Spirit: The Story Of Robert Frost*. She never saw the finished book.

My father had been gone since 1967, and my mother had often implied that I simply didn't understand her continuing sense of loss and loneliness. One morning, just after she had read the portion of the Frost manuscript in which I described Robert Frost's feelings after the death of his wife, Elinor, my mother looked up at me, her eyes brimming with tears, and said, "Oh, Natalie, you do understand!"

In *Breaking Tradition: The Story of Louise Nevelson*, which I began to write immediately following the publication of the Frost book, I described Louise Nevelson's anguish at the death of her mother, whom she adored. I was really writing about the still fresh loss of my own "bright and beautiful" mother, and exorcising some of my own grief.

Perhaps, years later, I was able to describe Thomas Jefferson's extraordinary relationship with his grandchildren precisely because I am so bound up with my own grandchildren and great-grandchildren.

It may be, to some degree, that we have to have experienced some of what we're writing about in order to be able to give to our work an intensity, a passion, that a work written in cold blood could never have.

I know that in my biographies I was better able to describe certain aspects of my subjects' lives as they related to my own. For only when a book is written out of passion will a reader respond with passion. I think of Robert Frost who said, "No tears in the writer, no tears in the reader."

4

Let's Pretend: Poems Of Flight And Fancy

From the time I was a little girl and my father read to me, I have loved the rhythm, the rhyme, the sound of poetry. Years later, as I searched for poems to include in a reading textbook that I had been asked to edit, a colleague suggested that I put together a collection of poems for young readers.

At just about that time my first grandchild was born, bringing with it untold joy, and ushering in a new period in my life. It also, quite by accident, expanded my professional horizons.

With the advent of Jody's birth, I found myself reading aloud once again the poems of my own childhood and those I had read to my children when they were little. I had a very receptive audience. Jody loved the sound of the words as I had – and as most young children do.

I remembered Robert Frost, who believed that the sentence sound often says more than the words. The way one reads a line or a word frequently makes a difference in the way one interprets its meaning. The sound was, for him, the most important part of poetry. "We write of things we see, and we write in accents we hear," he said. It is only when we read our writing aloud that we can tell if it's alive.

William Wordsworth, describing his childhood in his great autobiographical poem "The Prelude," recalled the time

> When first
> My ears began to open to the charm
> Of words in tuneful order, found them sweet
> For *their own sakes,* a passion and a power.

It is through *sound* that young children find their way to a poem.

As she grew, Jody came to love our poetry reading times together more and more. Her invariable plea as I finished reading a poem was, "Read another, Grammy!" I even went so far as to read some poems into a tape recorder, then mail the tape to Jody in Massachusetts, where she lived. I still remember reading a favorite of mine, Robert Louis Stevenson's "My Shadow," but first having to explain, on the tape, what a shadow is. Jody was three!

When Jody's sister Melanie (we called her Lani) was born, she loved poems too. Her favorite became "Binker," by A.A. Milne, and her wish was always, "Read it again, Grammy!"

Now I found myself becoming more and more steeped in poetry. I came to realize that poetry is truly the language of childhood. It says the most important things in the simplest way.

Ultimately, I took my colleague's suggestion that I compile a book of poems, and I began to look for patterns in the poems I was reading to my granddaughters.

I thought of what Jody always said when we were about to play a game: "Grammy, let's pretend...." I would call my book, *Let's Pretend*, I decided, and I would include poems of "flight and fancy," poems about "my inside-self," magical people, secrets, nature, animal friends, and poems of wonder. And I would write an essay on imagination, showing how "Let's Pretend" can be the passwords to the land of magic.

Poems that echo the longings, the wishes, the dreams of childhood in the rhythmic beat of its language can sing their way into the child's spirit and set aflame their imagination. By allowing them to use their *minds* to see, it provides a different way of seeing. Poems of the imagination, then, can become vehicles that help children view themselves and the world around them in a new way.

"A poem is a momentary stay against confusion," Robert Frost told us. "Each poem clarifies something." It is "a voyage in discovery" that "begins in delight and ends in wisdom."

Now my task began. I knew the title of the book, and I knew that I would include the poem "Binker," but what other poems would I include? How would I decide which ones to use? This is where the research - and the art - came in.

I gathered hundreds of poems before I made the final selection! I read in libraries, bought books, borrowed old out-of-print books from friends, even haunted out of print book stores, found magazines that published poems, and poured over my own extensive collection at home. I read them over and over. I learned that you get more from a poem each time you read it. One should never read a poem just once.

I found, also, that each poem had something different to offer – rhythm, rhyme, emotion, story. I made piles, then shifted the piles around. I added, I eliminated. I added more. I tried to find something that united them – that tied them together. I divided them into sections. Then I tried them out on Jody and on some of her young friends. They were five years old!

Reading poems to Jody and Lanie

Photo courtesy of L.H. Bober

Eventually, I decided that there would be six sections of poems: My Inside Self: "I'd like to change places"; Magical People: "I met a little elf-man once"; Secrets: "And all the playthings come alive"; A Taste of Nature: "I'm the one who woke the sun"; My Animal Friends: "Bee! I'm expecting you!"; and Wondering: "who knows if the moon's a balloon".

I had originally planned to dedicate the book to Jody, but by the time it was ready for publication, I had three granddaughters who loved poems.

The Dedication for *Let's Pretend: Poems of Flight and Fancy* reads:

For Jody
who took me back to the Land of Let's Pretend
and for Lani and Joelle
who keep me there

5

Once Upon A Time: An Enchanted Children's Bookstore

April 25, 1984 was a joyous day in our family that was to usher in yet another phase in my life. Once more, I would "come about," (change course, as in our sailboat,) and tack (sail) in a slightly different direction. On that day my daughter, Betsy, gave birth to her first child, and our third granddaughter. Joelle was a beautiful, tiny baby, but the circumstances surrounding her birth had been difficult, and I found myself driving from Manhattan, where we lived at the time, to Betsy's home in Westchester several times a week to help care for her.

When Joelle finally seemed to be "out of the woods," my husband and I decided to relax a bit on our sailboat, the "Restless Spirit," (which, incidentally, we had named in honor of Robert Frost; we called our dinghy "You Come Too" from Frost's poem "The Pasture"[3]). We left for a long weekend over the Fourth of July holiday. When I phoned my daughter from a dock one morning, she answered breathlessly:

"I knew you would call," she said. "I couldn't wait to talk to you. While I was walking the floor with Joelle on my shoulder last night, I had an idea. How would you like to open a children's book store with me?"

"Oh, Baby, let's do it!" was my instant response.

And so, eighteen months later, after studying and learning all we could, and in spite of much pessimism on the part of friends and family, we opened *Once Upon A Time, An Enchanted Children's Bookshop*. Ultimately, we proved that a mother and a daughter **can** work together happily and productively. It was a delightful interlude in my life, and helped me to see the field of children's literature from a totally different perspective.

Here I had an opportunity to meet highly regarded authors and illustrators who came to our shop to speak to the young people who were reading their books and, of course, to sign those books. Most importantly, I had the chance to read the books we carried – those we considered the best of the best.

---

3   I'm going out to clean the pasture spring;
I'll only stop to rake the leaves away
And wait to watch the water clear, I may:
I shan't be gone long. – You come too.

Inside Once Upon A Time
Photo courtesy of Jane Gelbard

At times, we were asked to review new books that were always becoming available. In this way I learned to differentiate between the good and the excellent. I had the opportunity to learn about books for children from "the other side of the coin."

What Betsy didn't know when she first made the suggestion - indeed no one knew - was that almost thirty years before, I had confided to my husband my longing to open a little bookshop that handled rare and scholarly books. But at that time in our lives it was financially impossible. Now I was able to use a small legacy from my mother to get us started. How pleased my mother would be if she could know.

6

Louise Nevelson: Breaking Tradition

Louise Nevelson's art spoke to me from the very first time I saw it. I had joined a women's study group in art history when my children were still quite young, and I was not working. One day, the group was viewing an exhibition of Nevelson's sculpture, and I became fascinated by the originality and beauty that she was able to create with simple pieces of wood painted black and arranged into unusual designs. Some were table-top size, many were large independently standing pieces.

Soon after I completed the course, I happened to share an elevator in the Waldorf Towers in New York City with a gentleman who was carrying a small, black wooden sculpture. I recognized it instantly as a Nevelson piece, and promptly fell in love with it. I never found out where he was taking it – nor to whom it belonged – but it seemed, in one small piece, to capture the essence of

Nevelson's work for me. The memory of it lingered, and haunts me still.

Several years later, a small chapel Nevelson designed, called the Chapel of the Good Shepherd, was being built in St. Peter's Lutheran Church within the Citicorp building, a soaring skyscraper on Lexington Avenue in New York City.

The author inside the Nevelson Chapel
Photo courtesy of L.H. Bober

I was working at a publishing house then, located just across the street from that building, and I was often teased about the amount of time I spent "meditating" in the Chapel. Actually, I was fascinated by the fact that the sculptures within the chapel managed to strike a delicate balance between religion and art, and that a Jewish artist from Russia had been asked to design a Lutheran chapel. Nevelson said of it, "We've broken barriers on both sides with this." And when the pastor of St. Peter's was asked why Nevelson had been chosen, he replied, "Because she's the greatest living American sculptor."

Out of my "meditation" evolved a selection on Nevelson entitled "Breaking Tradition" for a reading textbook I was editing at that time. Several years later I would write a book called, *Breaking Tradition: The Story of Louise Nevelson.*

I had already published biographies of two male poets, William Wordsworth and Robert Frost, and had decided that I really wanted to do a book about a female artist. I was considering the painter Mary Cassatt. When I went to the young people's library of the Metropolitan Museum of Art, and spoke to the librarian there, she immediately questioned my decision. Cassatt was a fine painter, she said, but much had been written about her.

"Why not do Louise Nevelson?" she asked. I was intrigued. I truly wanted to do a story about a female artist, and I already loved Nevelson's work. "Why not?" I thought. My decision was made.

Friends who knew of my desire to tell Nevelson's story invited me to a celebration in her honor at the Whitney Museum in New York City, and graciously introduced me to her. In spite of the accolades she was receiving, and the festivity swirling around her, she spoke to me briefly, and consented to my request for an interview.

Then my phone calls to set up an appointment went unanswered. I couldn't seem to get through to her. I continued to leave phone messages, none of which apparently reached Nevelson. Frustrated, I considered abandoning the project. How could I write about a living artist without interviewing her? The book would have no validity.

In despair, I made one final attempt. I had seen an obituary in the New York Times of someone I knew to have been her friend. I wrote a note of condolence, then held my breath.

One hot July morning in 1982 the telephone rang. "Hello Dahling, this is Louise." The lovely voice with its New England accent on the other end of the telephone startled me. Could it be? Could this be *the* Louise, the artist with whom I had been trying to arrange an interview for the past five months?

My persistence had paid off.

Now the day of the interview had finally come, and I was waiting with great trepidation for her to arrive at my apartment in New York City. I had alerted the door-man of the building so that he would recognize her – I couldn't be sure that he would know who she was – and phone to alert me that she was on her way up. Promptly at four o'clock, the elevator door opened and there she was!

She was dressed in a striking collage of clothes: open sandals but no stockings (in those days properly dressed ladies always wore stockings), a long Persian brocade skirt, a simple silk blouse, and her signature turban wrapped around her head. She wore no make-up on her smooth skin except for layer upon layer of enormous mink eyelashes that seemed to come in the door before she did. This tall, graceful, eighty-three-year-old woman swept regally into my apartment, stood in the entrance foyer, circled the living room with her eyes, and then, pointing with a long, elegant finger, announced, "I'll sit in **that** chair."

Instantly she became for me the queen I knew she had dreamed of becoming when she was just a little girl growing up in Rockland, Maine. She had chosen exactly the right chair: it had been my grandmother's. It was my treasure and it was where Louise Nevelson belonged.

As we sat in my living room, its broad windows overlooking Central Park, I felt a sense of awe that this larger-than-life artist was actually here.

In spite of myself, as she spoke, I began to relax. She spoke beautifully, and very softly, with the broad A of the New Englander. She had lived in Maine for fifteen years after her arrival from Kiev, in what was then part of the USSR. She had arrived speaking only Russian and Yiddish, and had learned English in school in Rockland. As she spoke, in short, clipped sentences, it occurred to me that just as her art was collage, so were her dress and her speech.

"Every time I put on clothes I am creating a picture," she told me. "I'm constantly creating. Why should I stop with myself?" She even talked like collage: putting words and phrases together, but seldom finishing a sentence.

But I was not prepared for her comment when, focusing on a photograph of my husband, she asked how long we had been married. My response shocked her. She asked, incredulously, "You've been married to the same man for thirty-three years? Dahling, isn't it boring?"

(As I write this I am still married to that same man – we have just celebrated our sixty-sixth wedding anniversary - and it has never been boring!)

Louise had married Charles Nevelson in 1920, after agreeing that they would have no children, then had a son Myron (Mike) in 1922, and separated from her husband in 1931. At that point she sent nine-year-old Mike to live with her parents and sister in Rockland, and went off by herself to Germany to study art with Hans Hofmann, a highly regarded artist and teacher.

She went on to tell me that for her there had to be what she called a "totality." Her head had to be clear, she said. Often, when she went to sleep at night, the forms she had been working on during the day would move around in her head as though they were people. "Now if I had had a mate there would have been intrusions – perhaps delightful, but intrusions nevertheless." Her love affair was with the wood. Her art was all that mattered. She had made the decision when she was still a child that she would be an artist, then sacrificed everything to make her dream a reality.

"I was like a horse with blinders on," she told me.

She then went on to tell me that for the five years she had lived in Russia she was always cold. And she hated the cold; and later, the bitter Maine winters. Somehow, though, she was comfortable in the art classroom at school. It wasn't until years later that she realized that she had generated her own heat in that room.

Suddenly we realized that three hours had slipped by and it was already seven o'clock. I phoned for a taxi for her, saw her downstairs, then hurried to relive our time together by adding to the brief notes I had taken as she talked.

Several weeks later my husband and I drove to Rockland, Maine, with the express purpose of seeing the environment in which Louise Nevelson had lived. The seacoast town is situated on a fine harbor and is rich in natural resources. As we drove around the countryside we saw the house she had grown up in on the poor side of town, as well as the seemingly inexhaustible stands of trees that sparked her creative mind. Rockland had been one of the major shipbuilding centers of the country.

As we drove around the area, I began to understand why Louise Nevelson had such an affinity for wood, and why most of her extraordinary sculptures were created out of wood. Suddenly, I could visualize her as a youngster collecting pieces of driftwood and bits of old lace – just as her father was collecting a warehouse full of antiques. And I could picture her accompanying him to look at – and learn about – the houses he was building. Her father worked hard, and had been able to buy land and a lumberyard, and work in real estate, contracting for and building houses.

Coincidentally, as I write this, I have just received an e-mail message from a niece, telling me that she and her husband were visiting the Farnsworth Museum in Rockland, Maine. The museum holds a collection of Nevelson's art, as well as some of her papers. The e-mail I received contained a photograph of a painting Nevelson had done when she was very young. It clearly portrays the influence on this child of the houses her father was building.

Even more fascinating for me were the vivid reds and greens she had used. The painting immediately brought to mind a story Louise had told me during an interview:

When I asked Ms. Nevelson how old she had been when she knew she would be an artist, her instant reply was "nine years old." Then she went on to tell me that when a librarian in the Rockland Library asked her what she wanted to be when she grew up, she answered, "I'm going to be an artist." Then she added quickly, "No, I want to be a sculptor. I don't want color to help me." Her unexpected answer frightened her so much that she ran home crying. "How did I know that when I never thought of it before?" she asked me.

Before my husband and I left New York for Rockland, I had written ahead to schedule an appointment to visit the Farnsworth Museum. I was particularly eager to see the art and the papers. When I arrived at the museum at the appointed hour the next morning, I was not prepared for the greeting I received. As I entered the museum I found the entire staff lined up, single file, along the banister on the stairway to the left of the main hall. Imagine my embarrassment when I learned that they were waiting to see what "a New York author" looked like! And I had hoped to be as inconspicuous as possible!

A lovely surprise, though, was a note that was waiting for me from Anita Weinstein, Louise's younger sister, inviting me to join her for tea in her apartment that afternoon.

Anita regaled me with stories about growing up with her older sister and brother, Nathan, as well as their little sister Lillian, the only sibling born in Rockland. I gathered many tidbits from her. First, she set me straight on Louise's place of birth. Louise had originally told me that she had been born in Kiev. Actually, Anita contradicted, all three children were born in the little "shtetl" town of Shushneky, not more than "a bend in the road," but not far from Kiev.

Anita told me a story about their childhood. On Friday evenings, the few Jewish homes in Rockland observed the Sabbath with the traditional customs and a special meal. After that dinner, Louise and Nate, as the oldest, were allowed to go to the movies. Anita was sometimes permitted to tag along.

On one such evening, Anita curled up in the theater seat and fell asleep. When the movie ended, Nate and Louise, still totally absorbed in the story of the movie, automatically got up from their seats, left the theater, and walked the mile and a half home. All the while they talked about the movie. When they arrived home half an hour later, their father was waiting up for them. He asked where Anita was. It was only then that they realized that they had completely forgotten about her. Isaac had to walk back across town, awaken the manager, and ask him to unlock the theater door. Anita was still sound asleep in the empty hall.

After a delightful afternoon, when I was ready to leave and standing at the door to say a final good-bye, Anita suddenly said, "Wait, Natalie, don't leave. I have something I must give you." Then she hurried into the bedroom and returned with a blue sweater in her hands. "I want you to have this," she said. "I made it – and it matches your eyes. And men like women in blue." She handed me a truly beautiful hand-made marine blue sweater that I loved instantly. I wore it for years, always thinking of her when I did, and finally gave it to a granddaughter who treasures it still.

During the course of my research, Nevelson granted me access to restricted material held at the Archives of American Art at the Smithsonian Institute in Washington, D.C. My dear friend, Dorothy Ehrich, accompanied me there to help sort through boxes and boxes of Nevelson's letters and photographs.

Large cardboard boxes of material were sitting on open metal shelves in a brightly lit room hidden away behind a large open public space. As we sat at a long metal table and began to sort through the material in the boxes, my friend said, "Nat, I can't do this. We're intruding on her personal life."

"But she's granted us permission," I reminded her with more assurance than I really felt. "And the material is here for all to see. She has given it to the country."

There were many touching letters from Nevelson's son, Mike, when he was a little boy living with his grandparents in Maine. One letter in particular moved us both to tears. In it, thirteen-year-old Mike thanked his mother for the gift of a tallis (a Jewish prayer shawl) that she had sent to him for his Bar Mitzvah. But, he told his mother, he would rather have her than the gift. He longed to see her. But his mother was busy painting in New York.

Later we came across a letter from Louise to a fifty-year-old Mike, reminding him to take his vitamins, eat liver, and take care of his feet.

It was then that I recalled being told by a friend of a telephone conversation that she had overheard in Mike's studio in Connecticut, when Mike was near sixty. He had responded to the caller, "Yes Mother, I've eaten. Mother, dear, I've had lunch. I *have* eaten." Only then could I begin to comprehend the relationship that existed between this mother and son – a son she had, for all practical intents and purposes, abandoned when he was only nine years old.

When my book about Nevelson was published, I sent a copy to her. She then phoned me to say how pleased she was with it and to ask if she might purchase a few copies for her family. I replied "No!" But, I told her, I would happily **give** her as many as she wanted, and asked if she would sign a few copies for my family. She graciously agreed, and asked that I bring the books to her home in New York City.

A few days later, as we sat at an immense polished black table in her dining room, signing copies of *Breaking Tradition: The Story of Louise Nevelson* for each other, she was still telling me of the terrible guilt she felt at choosing art over her child – and now her grandchildren and her great-grandchildren. But, said she, "They're so boring!" For someone like me, whose life is closely bound up with her children, grandchildren, and great-grandchildren, this was difficult to comprehend.

Being in her home was revealing on several levels. As she moved about, she was constantly rearranging objects on her tables. Everything was a "still life," she told me. Today, as I walk through my own home, I often find myself moving an object on a table ever so slightly – to make a better picture. And whenever I do, I think of Louise Nevelson.

She showed me the oriental rugs that she was stitching together simply "to keep my hands busy;" and the immense black sculpture standing against one wall that was ready to be shipped to the Tate Gallery in London for an exhibition. I could only think how privileged I was to be there to see all this and to know her.

As we were preparing to leave (a car had arrived to take Nevelson to a graduation ceremony at which she was to deliver a talk), she stopped into the powder room for a moment, then emerged saying "Oh, my dear, my hand shakes so I can't get my false eyelashes on straight anymore!" She was eighty-four.

Louise Nevelson was the only subject who was alive at the time I was writing about her. This created some unusual problems. Her priorities were very different from mine. I had to be extremely careful that the portrait I painted of her was in no way judgmental.

Even more constraining for me was the fact that Nevelson had an image of herself that she wanted to project, and I was seeking the truth about her. Always, as I write, I have in mind something written by Sir Sydney Lee, (1859-1926), editor of the *Dictionary of National Biography* in England, and known for his biography of William Shakespeare. He wrote, "The aim of biography is the truthful transmission of personality."

A good biographer is under oath to interpret the material she has gathered honestly. As I write, I try to create as truthfully yet as powerfully as I can, the world that is unfolding before me. If I paint a picture colored by my priorities, it is a false one.

Could I write what I saw as the truth about Louise Nevelson without offending or hurting her? And what is the "truth" about Louise Nevelson? How would her perception of herself align with my portrait of the artist?

Happily, as my research and writing progressed, I found, beneath the façade of Louise Nevelson, a warm and wonderful woman who had struggled for fifty-eight years to have the art world recognize her. For it was only in 1958, when she was fifty-eight years old, that she was invited by the Museum of Modern Art in New York City to participate in a show there.

She produced "Dawn's Wedding Feast," her first all white wooden assemblage.

Very quietly, this remarkable lady taught me much. She did what *she* wanted to do. Louise Nevelson's story is a lesson in perseverance, in a belief in oneself.

7

Marc Chagall: Painter Of Dreams

Marc Chagall: Painter of Dreams became the only book I didn't initiate. I was asked to do it on the strength of my previous books. So, when an editor at Jewish Publication Society asked me to write a biography of him, I accepted immediately. There was no question in my mind that I would like to spend several years with this extraordinary artist. I wanted to know more about him. This would be my chance to learn.

Marc Chagall's paintings had always fascinated me. They are different from the art of other painters whose work I know. Chagall seemed to me to be painting his dreams – looking for other possibilities – using his imagination as he searched for a different way to see.

To begin my research, the first book I chose to read was his autobiography, *Marc Chagall My Life.* The simple dedication, "to my parents/to my wife/to my native town" gave me clues as to what was important to him. The book itself told me what to search for.

As I read about him I learned that, as a child, he had listened to his uncle telling stories from the Bible. Then, later, perched on the roof of the house in the little village of Vitebsk, Russia, where he grew up, he read the stories himself and painted visions of them in his head. "I did not read the Bible," he said, "I dreamed it."

I began to wonder how much of his heritage was embedded in these stories. I wondered, too, about the wild emotion and ecstatic joy that are expressed in so many of these paintings. They are full of wit and humor. Where did this come from? What motivated him to paint a fiddler on the roof, a cow jumping over the moon, or a bride and groom floating over the rooftops? Here was my chance to learn the answers to these questions.

My portrait of Chagall would be painted against the canvas of history. As Chagall's life took him from Vitebsk and St. Petersburg in Russia to Paris, France, to Germany, back to Vitebsk, to America, and later to the south of France, his art reflected the history of the times as well as the influence on him of each of the places in which he was living at the time.

"The Rabbi of Vitebsk" was painted in that village in 1914. Chagall had been stranded there because of the outbreak of World War 1. In it he painted an old beggar whom he dressed in his father's prayer shawl, then dismissed him after half an hour because he smelled too much.

This beggar ultimately became "The Praying Jew," a haunting image and one of the greatest of Chagall's paintings. It ultimately became his favorite painting. For years in Russia he kept it under his bed to protect it.

Some years ago, when it was loaned to the Jewish Museum in New York City for an exhibition, I was privileged to view it. As I came upon it, I gasped. I had never seen anything like it. It took my breath away and brought tears to my eyes. It was a moment I would never forget.

Then, as I wrote about the irresistible joy that overtook Chagall in Paris as he painted his fantastic visions without stop – even through the night – it brought joy to me too. The City of Light, as Paris has often been called, was giving him a new way of seeing and expressing his familiar material. And I was gaining a new way of looking at art.

Like a whirlwind, Chagall moved from one trend in art to another. He saw the possibilities in all. What was different – what was special about Chagall – was that he interwove fact and fantasy. This is at the heart of all his work.

In the late 1930s, Chagall's art began to change. As I studied it – in books, in museums in New York and Paris, and in discussions with museum curators knowledgeable about Chagall's art, I began to realize how the persecution of the Jews by Adolph Hitler's Nazis was affecting Chagall. As the Nazis goose-stepped steadily toward World War II, Chagall's floating lovers, his flowers, his joyous colors were replaced by *isbas* (squat timber houses in Russia) in flames. His colors became harsher, his lines stiffer. He painted Vitebsk, his hometown, as a symbol of a suffering Russia.

Then I discovered a question that had to be answered. During an interview about Chagall with a knowledgeable curator at the Jewish Museum in New York City, I learned that Marc Chagall, a Jew, was buried in a Catholic cemetery in St. Paul de Vence in France. She showed me a video attesting to that. She had no idea why. I knew immediately that I had to find out! My husband and I made plans to fly to France. I would use the opportunity to find answers to this and to many other questions – and to learn more about Marc Chagall and his art.

Before we left for France we visited the grave of Marc's wife Bella, located not far from our home then in Westchester County, in New York. Bella, whom Chagall called "my nishoma," my soul, had died suddenly in 1944. The simple marble tombstone he carved for her is an eloquent testament to their love.

When, in conversation with the superintendent of the cemetery grounds, he revealed that a granddaughter of Marc and Bella, also named Bella, lived in New York City and frequently came to care for the stone.

This was an exciting piece of information. As soon as we returned home I located her telephone number and phoned her to request an interview. She agreed, and I found a delightful young woman who had obviously cared deeply about her grandfather. She provided me with an insight into Marc Chagall that would not have been available from any other person. They spent many happy hours together when she was a young art history major in Paris, she told me. She described walking hand in hand with him, always laughing a lot. "He made me feel alive," she said.

Several years later we even spoke about her illustrious grandfather on the same panel in Pinehurst, North Carolina. Happily, that relationship, formed over the interview at lunch at the Harmonie Club in New York City, continues to this day. Research takes many shapes – often serendipitous!

Indeed, my daughter serendipitously discovered Bella in her flower shop, "Fleurs Bella", in lower Manhattan. The shop is an obvious reflection of her grandfather's love of flowers. Marc Chagall always painted with a bouquet of flowers nearby to remind him of the chemistry of colors.

About one year after Marc's wife Bella died, the New York City Ballet asked Chagall to design the curtains, sets, and costumes for a ballet set to Russian composer Igor Stravinsky's "Firebird," based on a Russian folktale about a magical glowing bird. He decided to try. With Stravinsky's explosive music playing in the background, he painted an enormous curtain and three backdrops, and drew the designs for 80 costumes.

In 1989, when I learned that the City Ballet was about to stage a production of "Firebird," I phoned to ask if I might see the work Chagall had produced. The answer, happily, was "Yes!"

Thus, at the invitation of City Ballet's stage manager, we found ourselves seated in front center orchestra seats of the State Theatre at Lincoln Center in New York City (today re-named the David Koch Theatre) at eight o'clock one morning, photographing Chagall's work as it was being set in place. "Firebird" would open that evening.

The opening curtain is a bird-woman with outstretched wings soaring across a midnight blue sky. The final backdrop is a celestial wedding scene in reds and yellows, where the canopy, cakes, and candles explode joyously to the last chords of Stravinsky's music. Everything soars in Chagall's Firebird. And we were soaring as we left the theatre. This, too, is "research!"

Now we were ready to fly to France. I had written to Madame Valentina Chagall, Marc Chagall's second wife, who lived in France, to request an interview. She agreed.

We made Paris our first stop, where we were privileged to view the paintings by Chagall owned by the National Museum of Modern Art, Pompidou Center, some stored in their basement reserves. I had made arrangements by telephone for this visit before we left New York.

We visited the museum on a day when it was closed to the public. There, we were taken down to the basement where we watched as the curator drew out – one at a time – some of Chagall's paintings that had been stored away – paintings I had only read about but never seen. Seeing them "close up" made them somehow more real. They suddenly came to life for me. In fact, it became clear to me that what was unfolding before my eyes was the autobiography of Marc Chagall. His life's story was right there in his art.

The painting that made the greatest impression was the one Chagall and his then fiancée, Bella, had named "The Birthday." Seeing it from this vantage point, I could finally understand how Chagall had been able to transform everyday activities into miraculous happenings on his canvases. In this painting his simple room became a place where lovers could fly. Its story ultimately became an exciting segment in my book.

We visited the tiny studio on the outskirts of the city in which Chagall had worked. It was in a small round building called *La Ruche* because it resembles a beehive. It was there that Chagall met other Jewish émigré artists like himself: Jacques Lipchitz, Amedeo Modigliani, and Robert Delaunay, who would become one of his few close painter friends. He met the poet Blaise Cendrars and the brilliant poet and critic Guillaume Apollinaire. He was introduced into circles where literature, music, and painting went hand in hand. Exploring this relationship has colored my own understanding and appreciation of the ways in which the arts are intermingled.

We traveled on to Chartres to visit the famous cathedral there known for its magnificent blue stained glass windows. When Chagall was asked to create a cycle of stained glass windows for a cathedral in Metz, he began a collaboration with a master glassmaker. Here he quickly learned the technique of translating his designs into glass. Then Chagall visited Chartres to study its windows, and was moved by the brilliance of their blue, so like the blue in his own palette. But when we compared the windows at Chartres with Chagall's stained glass, we decided that his were an even more brilliant blue.

Back in Paris, at the Paris Opera House, we saw and were able to photograph the glorious ceiling decoration that Chagall had made for its vast (2,153 square foot) circular dome. The seventy-foot high ceiling, from which hangs a huge crystal chandelier weighing six tons, had been a great technical challenge to Chagall. But his doubts about whether he could accomplish this seemed only to stimulate his fantastic imagination.

The author on the grand staircase of the Paris Opera House
Photo courtesy of L.H. Bober

"Our dreams are only thirsty for love," he decided. He would breathe life back into this building. He conceived of the whole design as a flower with five petals, each with a dominant color to represent particular composers, and each to contain figures and symbols from the world of ballet and opera. It is an exquisite composition one does not easily forget. How fortunate we were to be able to look up at it - and to photograph it – from the vantage point of a seat in the orchestra of the magnificent opera house where we had gone to see a ballet.

Chagall's ceiling decoration at the Paris Opera House

We visited the Bibliotheque Nationale (the National Library) where we saw the original copy of La Fontaine's *Fables* (a French classic read by all French children) that Chagall had illustrated.

We visited Le Musée National Message Biblique, high on a hill above the city of Nice, overlooking the Mediterranean Sea. It was the only national museum in France at that time devoted solely to the paintings of one living artist. The paintings that hang there are Chagall's "Biblical Message." To see the museum – and his breathtaking interpretations of the Bible: "Adam and Eve in Paradise," "Moses Facing the Burning Bush," "Song of Songs IV," "Abraham Mourning Sarah," to name a few – in this setting - intensified the experience. And to speak to the Director of Education there added much to my understanding.

Now we drove south to St. Paul de Vence, adjacent to Vence, where Chagall lived the last years of his life. Here we experienced the light that had so entranced Chagall. We walked the narrow, winding, cobblestone streets of this little walled, medieval city that looks from a distance like a ship run aground on a hilltop.

Overjoyed that we were in St. Paul de Vence, and that Madame Chagall had agreed to see us, we looked forward eagerly to the prospect of meeting her, of seeing the inside of their home, and of learning why Chagall was buried in the Catholic cemetery there. This was particularly troubling to me because Marc Chagall had been a Jew – and a Jew whose paintings shine with an inner light of Judaism.

When I phoned to set up a specific appointment, I was told that Madame Chagall could not see me that week. "Call her next week," I was told. "But I'm only here for a

few days," I replied. "I return to America on Monday."
"Next week," the speaker repeated. Nothing I said could
convince her to see me sooner. I was devastated.

I soon learned from the innkeeper of the hotel
where we were staying that this was a common ploy
for Madame Chagall. Just a few months before she
had done the same thing to a journalist to whom she
had promised a story, and who had also come from the
United States. This was her way: She never said, "No."
She simply postponed meetings until they were impossible to keep.

That afternoon my husband and I climbed the steep
hills leading up to the Catholic cemetery, just outside
the town walls and overlooking the valley below. We
located Chagall's crypt. Most of the burial sites were
placed above the rocky ground. His was inscribed simply "MARC CHAGALL 1887-1985." There was nothing to indicate that Marc Chagall had been a Jew. As
I looked around at the crosses marking all the other
graves, I had a feeling that something was terribly
wrong. We placed two pebbles on the crypt (a Jewish
custom to indicate a visit and respect) and left quickly.

It was immediately apparent to me that I could not
leave St. Paul until I had an explanation for the Catholic
burial. Luckily, I have a very resourceful husband, and
a heritage from my mother of digging for material. We
were off on another treasure hunt.

My husband reminded me of the video I had seen
at the Jewish Museum in New York in which a rabbi
in Nice had indicated that a burial plot in the Jewish

cemetery in Nice had been offered to Madame Chagall but she refused it. "Why not track down that rabbi?" my husband asked. But how?

We decided, rightly, that there was probably only one synagogue in Nice, and found its address in the phone book. Off we went in our little car through the narrow streets of Nice, looking for the synagogue. But when we found it, it was locked – and not a sign of life.

The next day we returned to Nice from St. Paul de Vence, where we were staying. This time we found a worker in the synagogue. He spoke no English, but managed to convey to me in French that the rabbi could be found in an office above a ballet school on the next street. Wondering whether I had indeed understood his French, I walked there, located what seemed to be the building, and climbed the stairs. In a little office at the top of the staircase sat Le Rabbi.

In my hesitant French I tried to introduce myself and explain what I wanted. He never looked up from his work. I continued to talk. Suddenly, something I said must have pleased him and he was all smiles.

"Vous êtes juife ?" (You are Jewish?") he asked.

"Oui, Rabbi," (Yes, Rabbi) I responded.

He offered me a chair, apologized for his inability to speak a word of English, and phoned his wife, who, he told me, was fluent in English, to come to the office and interpret for us. But she, alas, was running off to meet the school bus. Then he promised to speak slowly, and proceeded to tell me a story.

When he finished, Rabbi Elkiess escorted me downstairs to where my husband was patiently waiting in the car, after driving through a maze of one-way streets, hoping he was in the right place. He really had no clue. He speaks no French. And it had taken him longer to drive around the one-way streets than it had taken me to walk – and disappear into a building.

Now, as the rabbi and I emerged from the building, the rabbi cried, excitedly, "Oh, Le Grand Rabbi!" Indeed, the chief rabbi of Nice, Rabbi Kling, who had been a good friend of Marc Chagall's, was just crossing the street and coming toward us. Introductions were made, and Rabbi Kling, who spoke English, promptly corroborated the story I had just heard.

This is the story the rabbis told me:

From the time he had settled in the south of France, Chagall had been a member of the small community of Jews in Nice. He had become a good friend of the rabbi of the temple and of the Chief Rabbi of Nice, as well as the Chief Rabbi of France. When the rabbis learned that Chagall was ill, they phoned and asked for permission to visit him. Madame Chagall refused.

A short time later, when the rabbis learned from a radio broadcast that Chagall had passed away, they telephoned once again to offer a burial plot in the Jewish cemetery in Nice. Vava Chagall refused even to take the call. Chagall's son, David, also heard of his father's death secondhand.

The only cemetery in St. Paul de Vence is the very small Roman Catholic one, where only longtime residents of the village have the right of burial. But once again, Vava's forcefulness asserted itself. Determined that her husband would not be buried in a Jewish cemetery in spite of his wishes, and eager for the recognition of being buried in this prestigious cemetery, she used much influence with the mayor of St. Paul to obtain a plot.

On the day of the funeral a gladdening spring sun shone over the little cemetery, transformed now into a dazzling garden of flowers. Hundreds of people were gathered from around the world. David stood quietly in the background during the short but moving ceremony. Nothing was said to indicate that Marc Chagall, whose Judaism had been such a vital part of his life, had even been a Jew. Then, just as the casket was being placed in the crypt, a friend stepped forward and recited the Kaddish, the Jewish prayer for the dead.

8

Thomas Jefferson: Man On A Mountain

Thomas Jefferson had always been a hero of mine. I had been collecting books and articles about him since childhood. I even had a file labeled, *Jefferson*. So when my editor, Marcia Marshall, returned from a meeting of the American Library Association and mentioned during a telephone conversation that there was a dearth of good biographies for the young adult reader about our early presidents, I was intrigued. When, aware of my interest in Jefferson, she suggested that I write his biography, I countered by saying, "Who am I to write about Thomas Jefferson? How can I compete with the scholarly works already in print? How dare I attempt to get inside the mind and heart of this brilliant "apostle of freedom?" At her urging, though, I promised to think about it. So I hung up the phone, thought about it for a few minutes, and phoned her back.

"I'll do it," I said. It was the best professional decision I ever made. It ultimately opened many doors for me, and introduced me to scholars who would exert tremendous influence on me and on my writing.

Thomas Jefferson was a rare blend of prophet and practical statesman, a reluctant rebel who saw the possibilities of the times in which he lived while at the same time recognizing the importance of the past. What made it possible for this young, wealthy Virginia aristocrat to lead his nation through a tumultuous period, to write words about freedom and equality that would ring out across the centuries and change the course of history, and to reshape his environment as much in his architecture as in his politics - yet remain a slaveholder? These were the issues I knew I must explore with particular emphasis on Monticello and slavery, in order to piece together all the disparate elements that made up the unique mosaic that was Thomas Jefferson.

Jefferson's mountaintop home that he designed. It was the first house in the country to have a dome.
Photo courtesy of L.H. Bober

As I was researching the life of Thomas Jefferson, reading and reading and reading about him, at one point I began to imagine myself with him in the State House in Philadelphia on

June 7, 1776, as a member of the delegation to the second Continental Congress. There Jefferson heard Richard Henry Lee resolve that "these United Colonies are, and of right ought to be, free and independent States, that they are absolved from all allegiance to the British Crown, and that all political connections between them and the State of Great Britain is, and ought to be, totally dissolved."

Soon, Jefferson was elected to head a committee of five to draft a document that would incorporate Lee's resolutions. He was nominated to "draw them [the articles of the document] up in form and cloath [sic] them in proper dress."

How would I describe how he wrote this critical document? As I attempted to accomplish this, writing and erasing many times over, constantly editing, changing, shifting a sentence or a paragraph around, re-thinking the way I said something, I suddenly realized that I was doing exactly the same thing that Jefferson had done more than two hundred years before – writing and re-writing. He called it "interlining" and copying it "fair." Remember, he didn't have a computer. He was writing by hand. I think of that chapter as the most exciting one in the entire book for me to write.

Jefferson worked on this Declaration of Independence in a new house on Market Street in Philadelphia, in which he had rented lodging. He wrote on a little desk that he had recently had made for him by Benjamin Randolph, a fine cabinetmaker in Philadelphia. As I read about it and studied pictures of this little writing box, I became possessed by a frenzy to see it. Jefferson had explained to Randolph that he wanted a travel lap desk convenient for writing that included an adjustable book rest for reading as well. It should be equipped with a drawer that could be locked, and within which he could store paper stock and written papers. It was to be fitted to hold supplies of ink, nibs for his pens, and sand for blotting. Mr. Randolph had been happy to oblige.

The multipurpose desk met all Jefferson's specifications and was a remarkable piece of furniture. Crafted of beautiful mahogany, it was as small as possible and lightweight, with a maximum use of space.

I decided to go to Washington, D.C. to visit the National Museum of American History, and arranged to meet Kate Henderson, the curator. She would show me the desk.

Once at the museum, Ms. Henderson escorted me downstairs to a bomb proof shelter in the basement of the building. She then went to a vault, unlocked it, and drew out a drawer in which rested an exquisite lap desk. It took my breath away. As I stood by, watching, I managed to ask hesitantly, "Could you take the desk out so I can see how it opens and what it contains?"

"Of course," replied the curator. "Just one moment, please."

At that point, she pulled on a pair of white cotton gloves and explained to me that our hands contained oil, which might streak the wood. I, gloveless, was not allowed to touch the desk. As she lifted the lid of this little writing box and opened its drawer, I marveled at Jefferson's brilliant and creative mind that had conceived its design.

**The desk on which Jefferson wrote
the Declaration of Independence
Photo courtesy of Museum of American History,
Smithsonian Institute**

I thought, then, about the Declaration of Independence and something I had recently read about it: "On that little desk was done a work greater than any battle, loftier than any poem, more enduring than any monument." Indeed, the desk is today considered the most important iconographic object in American history. And the Declaration remains the most profound document in the history of government since the Magna Carta, signed by King John of England in 1215, more than 800 years ago.

The desk was returned to its safe haven, and as we were proceeding back upstairs, I attempted to express my gratitude to Ms. Henderson for making it possible for me to view it. She replied with something that has stayed with me these many years: "I must thank *you*," she said. "I am in this job precisely because I love these objects. It is only when I can share them with people like you who love them as I do that I can enjoy them as well. It is your passion that makes my job worthwhile." I have never forgotten what she said. I try to remember that it is when we ask curators and librarians about that special book or precious icon that their jobs become more meaningful and pleasurable. This strikes me as similar to the goal of a biographer: sharing with my readers information I have discovered about the people whose lives I am studying.

I thought about the role of librarians again when I visited Colonial Williamsburg, the living history museum that represents the historic district of the city of Williamsburg, Virginia, in the eighteenth century. It was here that the sixteen-year-old Thomas Jefferson attended the College of William and Mary. And it was here that he was introduced to the philosophy of the Enlightenment, a pattern of thought that preached freedom of the mind, prevalent in Europe at the time. It was as I strolled Duke of Gloucester Street that the young Thomas Jefferson slowly came to life for me.

Williamsburg was also the place where the House of Burgesses, the governing body of the colony of Virginia in the eighteenth century, convened. It was on this visit to Williamsburg that we were privileged to view the *Journals of the House of Burgesses* at the

Colonial Williamsburg Foundation Library, and my husband was granted permission by the librarian to photograph a page in it. It was only as I read several of the pages that the people described in them – Patrick Henry, George Wythe, Richard Henry Lee - suddenly stepped off those pages and became real people for me.

And we visited the Raleigh Tavern, where the delegates to the House of Burgesses picked up their mail, and where Jefferson and his friends often danced at the balls given there.

Back in New York City, I visited the New York Historical Society to gaze for a long while at the portrait of Jefferson as president, painted by Rembrandt Peale in 1805, that hangs in a gallery there. As I absorbed the details of the painting – his eyes, his smile, his hair, his dress (the fur collar on his coat and the ruffled cuffs on his shirt), I realized that they revealed many important clues to who he was.

"I cannot live without books," Thomas Jefferson wrote to his old friend John Adams shortly after he had sold his splendid collection – some 6,700 volumes – to the Library of Congress. The original 3,000- volume congressional library had been burned by the British during the War of 1812. Jefferson considered his books to be "unquestionably the choicest collection of books in the United States." They covered the entire field of human knowledge, and he hoped they would have "some general effect on the literature of our country."

He used some of the money he received to pay off troubling debts, then immediately began assembling another library for himself at an astonishing rate.

It was when I was in Washington, D.C. with the express purpose of seeing the desk on which Jefferson had written the Declaration of Independence that I decided to visit the Library of Congress to see if there was a list of the books that had come from Jefferson.

When I introduced myself to the young lady at the desk and explained what I wanted, she immediately asked if I knew Dr. James Gilreath, Dean of Rare Books. He was a Jefferson scholar, she told me, and he had a young son. She was certain he would be interested in my project. She would ask Dr. Gilreath to speak to me. I thanked her and sat down at a table to wait.

Soon, a man appeared and said, "Mrs. Bober? I'm Jim Gilreath. How may I help you?"

I hesitantly began to describe to him what I was hoping to accomplish in my book. Soon we found ourselves agreeing that it was Jefferson's passion for books that so appealed to both of us and should be a major focus of the story I would tell.

Suddenly, Dr. Gilreath said to me, "I can see we're both on the same wavelength. Come with me. I want to show you something."

I followed him to the rear of the room where I watched as he opened a drawer of his desk, took out a key, which he then inserted into a small keyhole, barely visible in the wall behind the desk. He turned the key, and the wall swung away. Behind it was the room that housed the books Thomas Jefferson had given to the library so many years before! Today, those books are housed in a gallery of the new wing (built in 2008) of the Jefferson Building. We stepped inside and Dr. Gilreath took off a shelf and placed in my hands a book by the Roman historian Cornelius Tacitus, whom Jefferson considered the "first writer in the world, without a single exception." Jefferson was particularly taken with Tacitus's description, in his *Historiae*, of the privilege of Roman citizens to "think as we please, and speak as we think." Jefferson had had the book bound in leather with one page printed in Latin and the facing page printed in Spanish so he could compare the two languages. It was annotated in the margins in Jefferson's own precise handwriting. I trembled as I beheld it.

Two years later, when *Thomas Jefferson: Man On A Mountain* was published, I went to my publisher's office to sign some books that we would send, as a courtesy, to those wonderful librarians, curators, and researchers who had given of their time and expertise during the various stages of my research, and who were mentioned in my acknowledgments. As I contemplated signing a book to Dr. Gilreath, I recalled that he had a son who would be just about the age of the young people for whom my book was intended. On impulse, I picked up the phone and called him at the Library of Congress. I was put through immediately.

"Dr. Gilreath, I'm sure you don't remember me," I began hesitantly. " My name is Natalie Bober...."

"Mrs. Bober!" he interrupted. "Of course I remember you. Whatever happened to that book on Jefferson that you were writing?"

"It has just been published," I replied. "It is precisely the reason I'm calling. I would like to inscribe a copy to your son, but I don't know his name. Would you tell it to me, please?"

When we had established that his son was John, we went on to talk about the book and about Thomas Jefferson. Then I attempted to thank him for his kindness to me, and for the help he had given me.

"*You* thank *me*?" he queried. "Mrs. Bober, I thank *you*. You've made my day!"

I hung up the phone, then ran excitedly into my editor's office to repeat the conversation. "Can you imagine," said I, "the Dean of Rare Books of the Library of Congress of the United States of America just told me I'd made his day."

My dear editor responded with something I have never forgotten: "Perhaps, Natalie, at just this moment he is saying, 'Can you imagine, an author of a book on Thomas Jefferson has just sent an inscribed copy to my son!'"

Once again, I was struck by the realization that curators and librarians enjoy their jobs in relation to their ability to share the objects they care for with other people who appreciate them as they do.

As always when I am researching, I made yet another journey in my search for the real Jefferson. We traveled to Nimes, France, (from Provence) in the pouring rain, to view and photograph what Jefferson considered "the most perfect and precious remain of antiquity in existence," the Maison Carrée. In a letter to a friend he said that he gazed at it for whole hours, "like a lover at his mistress." Some years later, Jefferson designed the Virginia State capitol at Richmond, modeled on the Maison Carrée.

Le Maison Carrée
Photo courtesy of N.S. Bober

Exciting things continued to happen. After <u>Thomas Jefferson: Man on a Mountain</u> was published, my husband and I received a formal invitation to attend Thomas Jefferson's 250th birthday celebration at Monticello (which means "little mountain" and is pronounced the Italian way, Montichello), the home Jefferson designed for himself on a mountaintop 580 feet above Charlottesville, Virginia. The invitation we received read:

> *Th. Jefferson*
> *presents his compliments to*
> *Mr. and Mrs. Bober*
> *and requests the favour of his company*
> *to dinner on April thirteenth next*
> *at eight o'clock*
> *The favour of an answer is requested*
> *Black Tie*

We were included in all the festivities: At 7 o'clock in the morning we were at a groundbreaking ceremony at Shadwell, Jefferson's boyhood home, which had burned to the ground and was about to be re-built. Shadwell was so named in honor of the town in England where Jefferson's mother, Jane Randolph, had been born. Then, I was invited to speak at two schools in Charlottesville, one before and one after lunch. My husband uncomplainingly drove me to all the events, including lunch between the talks.

An afternoon ceremony, at which we heard Mikhail Gorbachev (president of the Soviet Union 1990-1991) speak of his reverence for Jefferson when Gorbachev was a student at the University of Moscow, capped the daytime events.

We arrived back at the Inn with just time enough to shower and change into formal attire for the evening. A final drive took us back to an extraordinary celebration at Monticello.

After alighting from the car, feeling very elegant indeed, we walked up the path toward the house, where Dan Jordan, then Director of the Thomas Jefferson Memorial Foundation, was waiting to welcome guests. While I stopped for a brief chat with him, my husband went ahead to pick up our seating cards.

When one of the ladies sitting at the table handed him our place cards, she asked where I was, and then queried, "And what do you do, sir?"

Larry, thinking of the then recent motion picture starring Jessica Tandy and Morgan Freeman, quipped, "Oh, I drive Miss Daisy." It wasn't long before that story had circulated throughout the entire two hundred and fifty guests!

As we wandered through the house, empty of tourists, we noticed several books on the mantelpiece in the dining room, and a chair nearby into which his grandson had carved Jefferson's initials. It brought home to us the realization that Thomas Jefferson was a man who never wasted a minute. He even read while he was waiting for his family to assemble for dinner.

When we strolled on the terrace with its majestic view of the lavender-tinted Blue Ridge Mountains in the distance, we had the sense that at any moment Mr. Jefferson himself would appear to greet us. We felt his presence there. And we felt, too, how fortunate we were to be there.

The author on the terrace at Monticello
Photo courtesy of L.H. Bober

Some months later another exciting invitation arrived, this one from filmmaker Ken Burns. I was asked to be a part of his forthcoming PBS television documentary on Thomas Jefferson. My biography, *Thomas Jefferson: Man On A Mountain*, I was told, (and I quote) "presented Jefferson in such accessible human terms that we felt your thoughts would help immeasurably in our struggle to know him." Consequently, I was interviewed on camera in my home by Camilla Rockwell, Ken Burns's co-producer. It was an experience I will never forget.

It was a hot July day, remembered particularly because we were asked to turn off the air conditioning throughout our house. The person controlling the sound was concerned that the noise might come through and distort my voice. We were asked to turn off the refrigerator as well for the same reason.

When those issues had been tended to, the crew turned its attention to setting the scene. First was the choice of a chair in which I would sit. But when the selected chair (my grandmother's!) was moved from the living room to our library, where our books could become the backdrop, I was asked if I would change my blouse to a different color. Fortunately, Camilla intervened with an immediate, "No, she can't!" She had guessed, correctly, that I had spent many days searching for just the right shade of blue.

The interview lasted about three hours, during which I was not permitted to look at any notes.

I also served as a consultant on the project, editing the manuscript as it arrived at my home in stages. Thus, I was given the opportunity to read and edit the screenplay as it was being written. Then, I spent an extraordinary two days in New Hampshire, where I viewed the film, and then discussed with the Jefferson scholars who had gathered there from all parts of the country the merits and deficiencies of the work. It wasn't until I arrived in New Hampshire that I realized that I was the only woman chosen as a consultant and a "talking head." The film was aired on PBS early in 1997. It continues to be shown periodically.

Undoubtedly, the most exciting result of my Thomas Jefferson biography occurred on the evening of February 11, 1997, when my husband and I were guests of President William Jefferson Clinton and

First Lady Hillary Rodham Clinton at the White House. We were there for a screening of the Ken Burns Documentary "Thomas Jefferson."

We arrived at the Visitor's Gate at 6:15 pm, and went through a security check (as at an airport). We then checked our coats and walked up the marble stairway to a hallway lined with red carpeting and flanked by an honor guard. The guard consisted of chosen members of all the armed services in full dress uniform, complete with ribbons and gold braid. As we walked the length of the honor guard, each young man greeted us with a warm smile and, "Good evening. Welcome to the White House."

At the end of the hallway we found ourselves in a reception area where a military orchestra, its members dressed in bright red uniforms, was playing selections from "The Sound of Music." They continued to play all evening.

We spent a dizzying hour in the reception area, watching the array of people arriving. We greeted Attorney General Janet Reno, who told us she was sorry she couldn't stay for the screening because she had urgent business calling her back to her office. We spoke at length to Pulitzer Prize winner Joseph Ellis and his lovely wife Ellen; to biographer Andrew Burstein and his young son Josh; to co-producer of the documentary Camilla Rockwell and her charming mother; to Dan Jordan, President of the Thomas Jefferson Memorial Foundation and his wife, Lou; to author Gore Vidal; and, of course, to Ken Burns and his two young daughters, among many others. During the rest of the evening I was constantly surprised by how many people recognized me and sought me out, since, as I stated earlier, I had been the only female talking head in the film.

At one point my husband slipped away, walked over to a Secret Service officer standing near the orchestra and asked if there were a telephone booth nearby where he might phone our daughter. (This was in the days before cell phones.) After ascertaining that she lived in New York, the Secret Service man reached behind him to a panel in the wall, behind which there was a telephone. He asked my husband what number he wanted to call, then repeated the number to an operator and handed the phone to him. When our granddaughter Joelle answered, my husband said, "This is the White House calling." My granddaughter was ecstatic.

At about 7:15 we were ushered into the East Room and seated in the first two seats off the center aisle in the second row. When I looked down, I saw the place cards on the seats of the two chairs directly in front of us: "The President" and "The First Lady." Large and small screens had been placed strategically about the room for viewing.

As we looked around the crowded room (one hundred and eighty guests had been invited to the screening) we saw members of Congress, industry, and the media.

Finally, the President and the First Lady were announced, the audience rose, and President and Mrs. Clinton came down the center aisle. The president escorted her to the podium, then took his seat. Mrs. Clinton graciously welcomed the guests and told us how delighted she was to have this presentation in the White House. She invited us to a Monticello supper in the State Dining Room following the screening, and affirmed that Thomas Jefferson did indeed bring ice cream to the United States. She then introduced Ken Burns, and took her seat in front of me.

Burns began to speak about Thomas Jefferson – what he meant to the country, and what he meant to Ken Burns. Jefferson was his hero, he told us, but that didn't mean that he was perfect. Heroes didn't have to be perfect. He described Jefferson as inscrutable, but called him the "Rosetta Stone" – the key to understanding our country. Then he said quietly, "Please roll the film."

Following the film, as we were ushered out of the East Room, we encountered waiters standing ready with glasses of champagne. Once inside the State Dining Room, we found a long buffet table set magnificently with a lavish and elegant menu. Waiters circulated carrying trays of tiny chocolate cups filled with vanilla ice cream topped with a tiny chestnut. A chocolate bust of Thomas Jefferson stood in the center of each tray. A table in the nearby Blue Room was set with an elaborate display of desserts. We were invited to enjoy the buffet and to stroll through any other rooms on the floor.

In the State Dining Room, the First Lady and the President were standing separately, welcoming anyone who approached to talk to them. I made my way first to Mrs. Clinton. She was charming, and I found myself engaged in a relaxed conversation with her.

The conversation turned to my writing and she asked if I would stop by the White House the following day to drop off copies of my biography of Thomas Jefferson and the newest one of Abigail Adams. Unless one could "override the ordinary channels," she told me, packages sent by mail often did not reach her. She then introduced me to her assistant, who arranged to meet me at the entrance to the White House to take the package from me and deliver it directly to the First Lady. This we did on the following afternoon – a Jefferson book inscribed to Hillary and William Jefferson Clinton, an Abigail Adams book inscribed to their daughter, Chelsea Clinton, and a thank you note for an extraordinary evening.

I was most impressed by the relaxed, informal atmosphere of the evening, a function, no doubt, of the Clintons' handling of it.

When I approached the President, he calmly included me in a conversation with two other guests, then praised my part in the film. When the conversation somehow turned to Sally Hemings, I said that I didn't believe that Sally had been Jefferson's mistress. It was inconsistent with everything we knew about Thomas Jefferson. But – we would never know for sure.

At that moment an attorney named Richard Cooley, who had come up behind me, and whom I didn't know was standing there, announced, "I know for sure. I'm a descendent of Thomas Jefferson and Sally Hemings."

Startled, I said I was doubtful, but "it's impossible to prove a negative." At that point, the President bent down to envelop me in a bear hug, saying, "I like that line!" He then went on to tell me what a wonderful job I had done in the film. It was quite a moment.

I was also introduced to Stephen Ambrose, author of *Undaunted Courage*, the story of the Lewis and Clark expedition. It was to be the basis of Ken Burns's next project.

Shortly after, Sharon Rockefeller, the wife of Senator Jay Rockefeller, sought me out and told me a story: Several weeks before, as she was preparing to leave for Paris to visit Pamela Harriman, then the American Ambassador to France and a highly regarded diplomat, Sharon had received a phone call from her.

"Has Ken Burns done a new documentary?" Pamela asked.

"As a matter of fact, he has," Sharon replied. "It's on Thomas Jefferson."

"Bring it with you," Pamela told her.

Sharon Rockefeller took the film to Paris and Pamela Harriman showed it to two hundred Frenchmen at the American Embassy. They loved it.

"The French think Jefferson is theirs, you know; he belongs to them," Sharon told me.

Sadly, Sharon, along with many others, would attend Pamela Harriman's funeral just two days later. She had died suddenly of complications from a cerebral hemorrhage.

9

Abigail Adams: Witness To A Revolution

It was 1986, and my son Stephen, a talented teacher of English and an American history buff, was reading the manuscript of my then work in progress, *Thomas Jefferson: Man on a Mountain*, chapter by chapter, and offering thoughtful and incisive suggestions.

One evening, I received a telephone call from him. "Mom," he said, "please listen carefully to what I have to say. Please hear me out. It is abundantly clear to me what your next book will be, but Abigail Adams doesn't move the Jefferson story forward at all. Take this section out. Don't throw it away," he cautioned. "Start a file, mark it Abigail Adams, and use it in your next book." And just so, *Abigail Adams: Witness to a Revolution* was born. Steve knew before I did that I was falling in love with Abigail Adams.

Early in my research, the first place I wanted to see was the parsonage in the little seaport town of Weymouth, Massachusetts, where Abigail had grown up. I made arrangements with the curator to visit the house, and to wander through it and photograph it.

I saw the narrow staircase just outside the parlor, where Abigail and her sisters would huddle quietly, listening to their parents and their lively and literate guests discussing the public questions of the times inside. The books on the shelves were those that Abigail's father, Reverend Smith, encouraged her to read, and often read to her. They included the works of William Shakespeare and the English poets John Dryden and Alexander Pope. They conveyed to a visitor the importance of learning to Abigail's father. The kitchen, with its spinning wheel and the cradle on the hearth helped me to feel the warmth and hospitality of this home.

What amazed me later on was to learn from the curator, and soon my friend, Hope Paterson, that I was the first biographer ever to request a visit to the parsonage. I have never been able to understand how anyone could write a story about Abigail Adams and not visit the house in which she was born and grew up.

I think of myself as a storyteller, but a storyteller whose facts are true. So I must be certain that the details – the facts I cite – are accurate. Early in my research on Abigail Adams, I was faced with a question that had to be answered. I had read two biographies of Abigail Adams, both written by respected biographers.

One described her as tall; the other said she was petite. How could I find out which one was correct? There are no photographs of her (photography had not yet been invented) and every portrait that had been painted of her portrayed her from the waist up.

Paintings of Abigail's husband, John Adams, showed that he was quite short and plump. It seemed important to me to know how she related to him in size.

One day, on a research trip to Peacefield, the Adams mansion in Quincy, Massachusetts, the last home Abigail and John had lived in, I discussed my dilemma with the curator of the house. She said, "Come with me and I will show you how you can solve your problem." She then took me to the second floor of the house, pointed out a large chest in the hallway at the top of the stairs, and suggested I open the top drawer. As I did, I noticed that the entire top of the drawer was a sheet of lucite. Under the lucite I beheld a beautiful full length dress from the eighteenth century, carefully preserved. Imagine my excitement when I was told that this dress had belonged to Abigail Adams. Looking at it, and measuring it, I could see that Abigail had been short. She was just five feet tall. Mystery solved.

One of the unexpected joys for me on that visit was discovering the roses that Abigail had brought home with her across the ocean from England more than two hundred and twenty-five years ago. They were in full bloom. Lilacs that she planted at the front gate after their return continue to welcome visitors to the house.

In this age of instant communication we sometimes lose sight of the fact that hand-written letters are the lifeblood of history, and for me as a biographer, they are the beating heart of biography.

When I first mentioned my desire to write a biography of Abigail Adams, I indicated that I would tell Abigail's story through her letters. The immediate reaction was that that could not be done – and besides – young people wouldn't read the letters! That was all I needed to hear. I love a challenge. I said nothing, but I knew exactly where I was going with this manuscript.

Letters give history a voice. No matter how much we think we know about a particular period in history, we always learn more when we read the letters of the people who lived at the time. The story of the American Revolution resonates much more deeply when we read its letters. Indeed, without letters we would know nothing about the extraordinary Abigail Adams, and would have only a picture of a vain, pompous (and misunderstood) John Adams. Their letters were the link that bound them together through their many years of separation.

Abigail's letters are her autobiography, and it was in these letters that she unwittingly displayed her remarkable intellect, her sense of humor, her talent as a writer, and her spirit as a person. It is the spontaneity of her expression that brings her and her times to life.

"My pen is always freer than my tongue. I have wrote many things to you that I suppose I never could have talk'd," she wrote.

One of my favorites was written just prior to her marriage to John: "The cart you mentioned came yesterday, by which I sent as many things as the horse would draw. The rest of my things will be ready the Monday after you return from Taunton. And then sir, if you please, you may take me."

Early in her marriage, as Abigail began to experience the long separations from John that would shadow and shape their marriage, letter writing became a way of life for her. Using her pen as an emotional outlet, she wrote extraordinary letters that recorded an extraordinary life.

From the time that John Adams was elected a representative to the Massachusetts Legislature, through his service to both the First and Second Continental Congress, and later as minister to France and then to England, and even continuing through his terms as vice president and president of the United States, Abigail and John read each other's minds as well as they read each other's letters across any extent of land or water.

Thus, what joy it was for me to find – and be able to purchase and read – *Letters of Mrs. Adams, Wife of John Adams*, two volumes, edited by their grandson Charles Francis Adams in 1840. It was the first collection of her letters to be published.

Later I sat in the elegant, wood paneled reading rooms of the Massachusetts Historical Society in Boston, The American Antiquarian Society in Worcester, Massachusetts, and the New York Historical Society in

New York City, where I was able to hold her actual letters in my hands.[4]

One delightful letter was sent to her Uncle Tufts in Weymouth when John Adams was vice president under George Washington and John and Abigail were living in Philadelphia. It was a fortunate find for me that gave me much information about the conditions under which she was living. Abigail asked her uncle to purchase "a sley" for her "for to go to market in winter, living two miles from it."

Reading her letters to her sister Mary was yet another experience that had a huge impact on me. They pointed up Abigail's intimate relationship with this sister, and made me feel so close to her, I could almost hear her voice.

Another serendipitous find came to me when I was attending a summer course entitled "Rare Books" being given at Cornell University, in Ithaca, New York. Lectures were often presented during our lunch period. One day I learned that Mary Beth Norton, professor of American history at Cornell, was delivering a lecture on Founding Mothers and Fathers. I hastened to attend.

It was at that talk that I heard Dr. Norton say, referring to Abigail and John Adams, "In fact, in her letters to John, Abigail began to refer to OUR farm or OUR house in Boston. Until then it had always been YOUR farm.

---

4   A historical society is an organization that collects, researches, interprets and preserves information or items of historical interest. Generally, a historical society focuses on a specific geographical area, or on a specific subject and the people involved.

John continued to speak of MY affairs at home. But both sensed the large measure of dependence he had come to place on her."

The more than 2,000 of Abigail's letters survive today as a written legacy to us because family members recognized their importance and ignored her pleas to "burn all these Letters least they should fall from your pocket and thus expose your most affectionate friend," as she wrote to her husband.

John's reply to her was, "The conclusion of your letter makes my heart throb more than a cannonade would. You bid me burn your letters. But I must forget you first." Their letters were the link that bound them together across any miles of land or sea over the many years that they were separated.

Throughout her life Abigail considered herself a "very incorrect writer." She agonized about her handwriting, her spelling, her pointing (punctuation). She never seemed to realize that, in spite of this, her keen mind and her ability to express ideas poetically shone through all her letters. Indeed, not only do they serve as her autobiography, but they show us the human side of the American Revolution.

As I read those letters I found myself with her in Boston on a cold, clear night in March of 1770, as she coped with two small children while the explosion that came to be known as the Boston Massacre was taking place outside her window.

I felt her terror as Massachusetts was plunged into the fierce tumult of the American Revolution, and every alarm sent minutemen marching past her door, hungry, thirsty, looking for a place to rest.

The Braintree house today

Braintree House where John Adams had been born, and where he brought Abigail after their marriage.
Photo courtesy of L.H. Bober

I smiled as she described little seven-year-old Johnny proudly marching back and forth with the soldiers drilling in the field behind her house.

I listened as she taught him how to read and write, and subtly began to inculcate in him a sense of duty to his papa and to his country.

I walked with her and John Quincy to the top of Penns Hill to witness the Battle of Bunker Hill, and to watch Charlestown burning in fires set by the British troops. Then I sat with her as she wrote to her husband, at that time a delegate to the Continental Congress in Philadelphia:

"The day, perhaps the decisive day is come, on which the fate of America depends. My bursting heart must give vent at my pen.... Charlestown is laid in ashes."

Her bursting heart often found vent at her pen, and we are the richer for it.

I sat with her on lonely nights when, in the silence of her cold, dark house, using her pen as her emotional outlet, she wrote letters to her husband pouring out her fears as well as her passionate love for him.

As I found myself sitting at my desk with her in the quiet of my own house, often at two o'clock in the morning, I could understand how Abigail claimed that time as hers, time after the children were asleep and her chores were done. I understood, and empathized, when she wrote: "There are particular times when I feel such an uneasiness, such a restlessness, as neither Company, Books, family Cares or any other thing will remove, my Pen is my only pleasure."

Recognizing the potential importance of their letters, John asked Abigail "to put them up safe and preserve them. They may exhibit to our posterity a kind of picture of the manners, opinions, and principles of these times of perplexity, danger, and distress."

They do just that – and more. For me, the years that I spent reading and re-reading them have been an education and an inspiration. They have taken me on a journey back in time. Indeed, Abigail Adams has never been surpassed as a chronicler of domestic events and manners. She bequeathed to us the rich legacy of her life, her thoughts, and her emotions.

The opportunity to live, even temporarily, in the eighteenth century, to immerse myself in the period, the happenings, and the people – and to write about them – was my flight from issues surrounding me. But from that came an award winning book, a highlight of my career.

My husband and I had visited our eldest granddaughter, who was a counselor at a camp in the Adirondack Mountains in upstate New York. We made the four-hour drive home in a fierce thunderstorm, and arrived at our house well past midnight. As we grudgingly listened to our telephone messages on our answering machine, almost too tired even to hear them, we suddenly came to life.

"Hello, Natalie, this is Marcia," the quiet voice of my editor said. Then the excitement burst through her normally restrained demeanor as she continued, "I've just received word on my E-Mail that *Abigail Adams: Witness to a Revolution* has won the Boston Globe/Horn Book Award for the Best Non-Fiction Young Adult book of 1995. Congratulations!" The message continued, but I heard none of it. I had to re-play it later. I was in a state of shock. What an emotional roller coaster this day had been!

I reflect now on the many awards and fine reviews that *Abigail Adams: Witness to a Revolution* has garnered, and I think about how women today are still being torn by conflicting loyalties. Yet our lives are longer and filled with more possibilities than ever before. And perhaps it was Abigail Adams who was among the first to open the door to these possibilities. From the time she was a child she agitated for the opportunity to go to school, and continued to push for the right of women to an education. She campaigned for the right of women to vote, and fought for them to be given the same legal status as men.

During my research, by reading many of the more than two thousand extraordinary letters of Abigail Adams that survive, I was given that rare privilege every biographer yearns for: a glimpse into the mind and heart, and even into the soul of her subject.

10

Countdown To Independence

"Who shall write the history of the Revolution?
Who can write it?
Who will ever be able to write it?"
John Adams to Thomas Jefferson, July 30, 1815

King George III of England was a tyrant with wicked plans to do away with the British constitution, which guaranteed liberty to millions of people. These plans were foiled by the courage and resistance of a small group of rebels in the American colonies. He was a corrupt monarch who, in attempting to restore the divine right of monarchy, instead lost the most precious jewel in the crown of the British Empire.

Or **was** he? I had to find out.

My grandmother, who was a constant presence in my life as I was growing up, had grown up in England during the reign of Queen Victoria (1819-1901), granddaughter of King George III.

It was she who kindled in me a love of a country I had never seen, as well as a desire to learn as much as I could about it. All through school, as I studied English and American history, I wondered why the American colonies had separated from England. How had the American Revolution come about? What was England like in the eighteenth century? Was George III truly a tyrant? Who were his ministers in Parliament? In the New York City schools that I attended, George Grenville, Charles Townshend, and Lord North were portrayed as villains who had lost the American colonies. How could they have done this? Were they really villains?

Then, as I researched and wrote biographies of Thomas Jefferson and Abigail Adams, two Americans intimately connected with the colonial period, my curiosity was piqued even more. My two younger granddaughters, Joelle and Melanie, both of whom love history, began to ask similar questions. Finally I decided that the best way for me to find the answers would be to delve deeper into the pre-revolutionary period and write the story of what had actually happened.

I have always felt that writing is exploration. I write to learn. My drafts become a lens helping me to see my subjects from a new perspective. I decided to apply that philosophy to study the period from 1760 to 1776 – on *both* sides of the Atlantic Ocean. Perhaps I might discover a story worth telling. As I wrote, I promised myself, I would keep in mind the understanding that writing history is a craft, but at its best it can be an art form. I would use the skills I honed as a biographer and tell my story through the eyes of the people who made it happen.

First, I would ask the questions: Who were these people? Who were the key players in the thirteen colonies? Who were the key players in England? What forces were at work that swept them into a conflict that precipitated a shocking revolution and severed the ties between Britain and her American colonies?

And I would remember what John Adams wrote in a letter to Thomas Jefferson on August 24, 1815:

"As to the history of the Revolution, my ideas may be peculiar, perhaps singular. What do We Mean by the Revolution? The War? That was no part of the Revolution. It was only an Effect and Consequence of it. The Revolution was in the Minds of the People, and this was effected, from 1760 to 1775, in the course of fifteen Years before a drop of blood was drawn at Lexington."

To begin the search for answers to my questions I was fortunate to discover that a one-week summer course was being offered at Harvard University by British historian Peter Griffin and American historian Mark Peterson, entitled "In Defense of the Crown; In Defiance of the Crown." I enrolled immediately. The course was all I had hoped it would be. In a series of debates between the Englishman and the American the contrasting views of the British people and the colonists were brought into sharp focus. The course provided exactly the background I needed to set me on my way. An added bonus was the opportunity to carry on discussions with classmates in a social environment after class each day.

It was Mark Peterson who recommended that I interview distinguished American historian and Harvard University professor Bernard Bailyn, who reinforced my desire to look behind the scenes to find the story behind the story. It was he who recommended that I read the letters of Thomas Hutchinson, which ultimately proved invaluable. Indeed, a year later, sitting at a desk in the famed British Library and reading those letters helped me to better understand the relationship between Thomas Hutchinson, royal governor of Massachusetts, and Sam Adams, known as a behind the scenes molder of actions for the colonists. It was Professor Bailyn, too, who impressed upon me the importance of linking the intellectual developments of the time with the social and political developments. It helps explain how we got where we are, he told me. We must present the past in the context of its own time, somehow disengaging it from our present time. We cannot look at the eighteenth century through a lens ground in the twenty-first century.

Once again, I would be living in the eighteenth century, this time with an amazing cast of characters, both in England and the American colonies.

But I had to get to know all these characters well enough to bring them alive for my readers. The only way to do that was to begin a methodical program of reading individual biographies of each one, as well as histories of the period, both in the colonies and in England. Indeed, to learn the British point of view would be essential. And – I would have to travel to England, as well as to Boston, Massachusetts and Williamsburg, Virginia.

On one of those trips to England, in conversations with teachers of history there, I became aware that the loss of the colonies was hardly mentioned. As I searched in vain for books that discussed this period, I came to realize that the British would prefer to forget about this time in their history. They are not proud of it.

It was on that trip that we took along our eldest granddaughter, Jody, who, with my husband, spent a delightful morning touring London on one of its famed double decker buses while I continued my research in the British Library.

I think back now to one of my adventures on my own, a two week stay at a charming inn in Yorktown, Virginia, just a short drive every day to and from Colonial Williamsburg, a re-creation of the eighteenth century town exactly as it had appeared then. It provided yet another important phase in my research. First, there was the village for me to stroll in, including all the many craft shops, exactly as they had appeared then.

In addition to the shops there were the libraries, museums, and book stores, the College of William and Mary, and the scholars always happy to share their knowledge. And there were Bill Barker, who every day "became" Thomas Jefferson, and Jack Flinton, who brought the character of John "the Tory" Randolph to life for me.

I am reminded, too, of the wonderful people who kept watch over me there, as well as the deeper under-standing of my subject that I gained. On the weekends much loved niece and nephew Lisa Ehrich and Dr. Robert Bernstein and their three delightful daughters, Allison, Emily and Jill, visited from their home in Norfolk, Virginia, making those days most enjoyable. And spe-cial friend Brenda La Clair, then Director of Education at the DeWitt Wallace Gallery in Williamsburg, whose parents had been killed in an automobile accident, lov-ingly followed me back to the inn in the evening to be certain that I arrived there safely.

I had brought along my lap-top computer and trust-ed mini-printer, and was thus able to work in the large and very comfortable accommodation I had at the inn. I could type away in the evenings, after spending my days absorbing the plethora of material available in Colonial Williamsburg.

Come back with me now and consider my original question: Was George III a corrupt monarch – or was there another side to him? Who was George III? Let's find out.

On Saturday morning, October 25, 1760, the young Prince of Wales, George William Frederick, set out on his morning horseback ride. Shortly after, he was overtaken by a messenger who brought sad news. His grandfather, King George II, had died.

The prince's father had died in 1751, when the prince was just twelve years old. Now, at twenty-two years of age, Prince George was heir to an empire.

George had been a shy and silent young boy with no friends his own age except for his younger brother, Prince Edward, to whom he was deeply attached.

From his father he had inherited an intellectual curiosity and a love of art and science. With his father's death, the adults around him became so concerned about his future as king that they forgot about the growing boy. When George turned seventeen, he became the student of John Stuart, Earl of Bute. Bute, as he was called, became George's tutor and friend. But he strove to teach a boy how to become king by seeking the answers in books. He was unable to guide the young George in how to deal with people.

Although George had not learned to read fluently until he was eleven, he developed a passion for books and had begun to collect them. What had not been provided for were his emotional needs.

From my reading I learned that George III ultimately became a beloved and popular king. Even the American colonists at one time called him "the best of kings." Then why, in the Declaration of Independence, did Thomas Jefferson brand him as "unfit to be the ruler of a free people"?

Jefferson did so because he understood that the colonists were **not** rebelling against established political authority, but were a free people maintaining long established rights against a usurping king. Those rights had been granted in the Magna Carta, the great charter of the liberties of England, and considered one of the most important legal documents in the history of democracy. During the American Revolution, Magna Carta served to inspire and justify action in liberty's defense. The charter had been signed by King John on June 15, 1215, in a field at Runnymede, England.

Through my reading I also learned that George III can well be considered the most cultured monarch ever to sit on the throne of Great Britain. He was a lover of art and a book collector who started the esteemed British Library. To see that library in London can take your breath away. For me - to have my own library card, to be able to walk into the library early in the morning, before it was opened to the public, to sit in those surroundings and read the original letters to and from Thomas Hutchinson that Professor Bailyn had recommended, was most enlightening.

Once again, as she had so many years before when I was researching the life of Robert Frost, my editor had given me a letter attesting to the fact that I was a scholar from America who was researching the period in England from 1760 to 1776. It opened many doors for me and made my research all the more focused and exhilarating.

At that point in my research, the British Library was still a part of the British Museum, occupying the circular museum reading room. Several years later the library moved into a new building in a different part of London. It was in that new building that I saw the Magna Carta.

How exciting it was for me that it was my then teen-age granddaughter Joelle, who spent her summer of 1998 working with me on this project, discovered the announcement of the death of King George II in the *Boston Gazette* of January 1761 at the New York Public Library. What a joy it was to have her, and, later, to watch as she meticulously created the cast of characters and the chronology for this book, helped with reference notes and bibliography, and searched out pertinent material about eighteenth century London. She was becoming a researcher!

I took particular pleasure in the time that I discovered my granddaughters Joelle and Melanie, both of whom share my love of history and passion for writing, reading the manuscript aloud to each other during a snowy week in the tiny town of Rensselaerville, NY. Later, they honestly and lovingly articulated its strong and weak points, helping me to see it through their eyes. Their ability to express the philosophy behind their suggestions, and even to recommend some necessary changes, was extraordinary. It is they who keep me writing.

And speaking of family, once again it was my son Stephen who, as a talented writer, teacher and lover of American history, fueled the fire of my enthusiasm for the eighteenth century. His walking me along the Boston "Freedom Trail," commenting as we went about the relevant importance of the sites we visited, was invaluable. It was he whose suggestions throughout triggered many significant additions and changes.

Let's look at some of the other questions I tried to answer for my readers: In the American colonies, in Boston, Massachusetts, how did a shy, good natured young man named John Singleton Copley, considered today one of the finest American portrait painters, try, single-handedly, in an amazing moment of courage, to stop a revolution?

Actually, I had never known that Copley played a part in this story. I knew only that I love the portraits he painted. But a chance reference to a newspaper article in the *Boston Gazette* of December 1773 – and then locating that article — led me to what became for me a fascinating story – and a chapter in my book.

Copley's friend Paul Revere was the trusted express rider who alarmed the countryside on the night of April 18, 1775. Revere twice rescued John Hancock and Sam Adams from the British, and saved the secret papers of the revolution. And –I discovered that his dog played an important role as a messenger that night:

Just before Revere was to be rowed across the Charles River toward Lexington to warn the colonists of an imminent attack, he discovered that he had forgotten his riding spurs. So he hurriedly wrote a note to his wife, tied it to the collar of his faithful dog, who had followed him to the spot, and sent him home. Soon the dog returned with the spurs in place of the note.

Revere's blunt, capable hands fashioned some of the most beautiful silver in the colonies. He often made lovely silver frames for the miniature portraits Copley painted. Some of those portraits that would be reproduced in my book resulted from this research.

Paul Revere's engraving of what Sam Adams named the "Boston Massacre" served as an inciter to the Patriots. Sam Adams was the radical behind the scenes instigator of revolt. Yet he worked tirelessly for independence by letter writing and organizing political meetings. And it was he who inspired a new spirit of harmony when the rebel colonists met at a Continental Congress four years later.

When it was proposed that the sessions of Congress be opened with a prayer, the delegates thought it impossible to find a prayer agreeable to all. There were many different religious sects in Congress. But Sam Adams was ready. In a brilliant piece of strategy, he suggested that a Church of England clergyman from Philadelphia lead the prayer.

The delegates were startled. They knew that Sam Adams was a stern Puritan and a critic of the Church of England. But Adams assured them that he "could hear a prayer from a gentleman of Piety and Virtue who was, at the same time, a friend to his country." His proposal inspired a new spirit of harmony.

The loyalist Thomas Hutchinson, then royal governor of Massachusetts, was perhaps the most tragic player on the stage in this drama. He was a man who genuinely loved Massachusetts. He had been born and brought up there. Yet, he was ultimately forced to sail to England, never to return to the colonies. Why?

Was Sam Adams one of those responsible for the vicious destruction of Hutchinson's house and all its contents, including all his notes for a history of Massachusetts that he had been writing?

Hutchinson's stubbornness ultimately triggered Sam Adams's signal to dump the tea in the harbor, in what we have come to call the Boston Tea Party.

Sam's short, plump, and scholarly second cousin, John Adams, then an obscure young lawyer from the little town of Braintree, Massachusetts, had said as a very young man, "I want to do something that will surprise the world." Then, with the help of his extraordinary wife, Abigail, he went on to do just that.

John Adams was a true Patriot, yet he defended the British soldier who had been "Captain of the Day" on the night of the Boston Massacre, and was then accused of murder. John Adams was a strange revolutionary. He believed in rule by law. The accused have a right to legal counsel, he said. A fair trial would be proof to the British that the colonists believed in preservation of constitutional rights. If the soldiers killed in self-defense, they deserved to be acquitted. He would say, many years later, that it was "one of the best pieces of service I ever rendered my country."

And who were the other players in this drama in London? I learned a great deal from Jeremy Black, distinguished professor of eighteenth century British history at the University of Exeter in England. I had first met him at a symposium at the University of Virginia some years before.

And - in my reading - I met many of these players:

William Pitt, a dynamic member of the House of Commons and a staunch friend of Britain's American colonies, had played an important role in the unfolding drama. Pitt provided a sense of vision, a steady nerve, and an iron will. He had earned for himself the title "The Great Commoner." The people trusted and loved him.

He was considered the most brilliant war minister in British history, yet in the end, his advice and his strategies were not heeded.

I would have to learn why not.

I would have to explain to readers the bold and fateful policy of a man named George Grenville. He insisted on dealing with what he called "the American problem" in his own way, thereby sowing the seeds of a revolution.

And I would have to describe the role that was played by Charles Townshend, a brilliant but unscrupulous, flashy, young politician who was known as "Champagne Charley."

Teapot denouncing the Stamp Act
Photo courtesy of L.H. Bober

Many young people studying American history memorize the facts that the Stamp Act was passed in 1765, and the Townshend Acts in 1767, but they have no idea who proposed the Stamp Act or why – nor do they really understand who Townshend was and what the issues were.

Many know little about Lord North, the prime minister whom King George was certain could subdue the colonies. North's moral character, his wit and good humor, and his solid intellectual abilities commanded respect in Parliament. Yet he was hated by the colonists.

There's a wonderful story that's told about him: Often there were long debates that took place in the House of Commons. Lord North would tilt his large head back on his seat and doze off while the speaker droned on - frequently for hours.

On one occasion, when George Grenville embarked on a lengthy speech on finance, North said to a neighbor, "Wake me up when he gets to modern times." When his neighbor eventually nudged him, North listened for a few minutes, then said loudly, "Zounds! You have waked me a hundred years too soon!"

At another time, North closed his eyes while a member of the opposition was speaking. When the speaker complained that the Prime Minister was asleep, North, in a stage whisper, murmured, "Would to God I were!"

One of the most remarkable characters I would meet in my research was Benjamin Franklin. An American who spent many years in England, he played a significant role in the repeal of the Stamp Act. Franklin's prime objective during those years was to bring the two parts of the empire together in friendly understanding. His opportunity came when he was ordered to testify before the House of Commons on February 13, 1766. British merchants and visiting Americans had been invited to listen.

In a good-humored and carefully rehearsed performance, with a wealth of facts at his command, and an ability to answer without offending the questioner, this philosopher, dressed in a simple brown suit, introduced himself simply as "Franklin of Philadelphia," then stood before the members of the House of Commons and put forth his country's position clearly and logically. He remained standing for four hours, responding to more than one hundred and seventy-four questions. It was a brilliant performance.

Reading it was one of the highlights of my time at Harvard. I still enjoy re-reading it from time to time. It reminds me of how critical preparation and diplomacy are to success.

These were some of the questions I had to address. In searching for answers, I filled four notebooks with pertinent material, and realized, once again, that history has many interesting stories to tell.

I wrote earlier that for me the joy of research is to think and to learn. And as I researched and wrote *Countdown to Independence* – over a period of five years – I accomplished my original goal. I found myself able, finally, to understand how the colonists came to a decision to separate from their mother country – and how the English provoked this decision.

I gained an insight into the personalities of the key players on both sides of the Atlantic Ocean. Most importantly, I gained a better perspective on the true meaning of words that today we take for granted: freedom and democracy. I resolved for myself issues and questions that had been haunting me since I was a young student.

I was even able to imagine myself in the eighteenth century on the day we spent entirely on the eighteenth century floor of the Museum of the City of London. It was only then, when I saw the gold coach made especially for King George III's coronation in October 1761 that I realized fully what the pomp and pageantry must have been like. That magnificent coach took the newly crowned king and his queen from the coronation ceremony at Westminster Abbey to Westminster Hall for the celebration. It was on that trip that the great diamond fell out of King George's crown. Fortunately, it was quickly found and restored. It can be viewed now in the Tower of London, along with all the magnificent jewelry of the kings and queens that has been amassed over the centuries.

I often tell people that I live part of my life in the eighteenth century. For me, the opportunity to immerse myself in the period, the happenings, and the people, has been the reward of a career that has granted me fulfillment and untold pleasure.

11

Thomas Jefferson: Draftsman Of A Nation

A Second Look/A Second Book

In 1891 historian Henry Adams observed about Thomas Jefferson: "A few broad strokes of the brush would paint the portraits of all the early presidents with this exception … Jefferson could be painted only touch by touch, with a fine pencil."

Over the past years much new scholarship has allowed "a few more strokes" to be added to the portrait of Thomas Jefferson "touch by touch."

In November 1998 the results of DNA testing concerning a possible relationship between Jefferson and his slave Sally Hemings appeared in <u>Nature Magazine</u>, and set in motion new probing. One good effect that may have resulted from this DNA testing is that scholars were stimulated to take another look at *all* the available evidence, and to view that evidence sensitively and carefully – particularly noting black oral history. Black oral history – ignored in the past – can provide an important perspective on the complex relationship between a slave owner and those he owned.

In the past there had been an unwillingness to accept the story handed down through generations of Hemings family members, that Madison Hemings was the son of Sally Hemings and Thomas Jefferson. I and many other historians were guilty of accepting this view.

Richard Cooley's statement to me at the White House in 1997 that he was a descendent of Thomas Jefferson and Sally Hemings stayed with me and haunted me for several years. It may well have been one of the reasons I eventually decided to have another look at Thomas Jefferson's life. Due to all the new information that was unfolding, I had begun to change my mind about Jefferson and Sally Hemings, and felt I had to write another biography of him.

Then, in June 2000, I attended a five-day symposium at the University of Virginia entitled "Jefferson and Slavery," where Jefferson scholars attempted to take another look at the available evidence concerning Jefferson's stand on slavery and race and to put it all into perspective. There, as my mind slowly began to adjust to the possibility of a different view of Jefferson as a slaveholder, I began to question my – and other scholars' – conclusions.

It was at this time that leading Jefferson scholar Peter Onuf, Jefferson Memorial Foundation Professor of History at the University of Virginia, happily shared his wealth of knowledge with me and sharpened my focus on Jefferson and slavery over pizza in a tiny café in Charlottesville, Virginia, just as he had done before, on a sunny afternoon on the lawn at Oxford University. They were experiences I knew I would never forget.

A subsequent visit to my granddaughter Melanie's college class, in which Annette Gordon-Reed's book *Thomas Jefferson and Sally Hemings: An American Controversy,* was being discussed, reinforced my feeling that I must take a deeper look at Thomas Jefferson and slavery. I must start over again. I must look at *all* the evidence. I must take my readers into Jefferson's world. I owed that to them – and to my granddaughter.

My main reason for a second look was my own need as a historian to revisit Jefferson's story in order to better understand and address the controversy raging around him, to reassess his role in history, and to consider his relationship to us today.

Out of the UVA conference and my class visit emerged my decision to write a new biography of Thomas Jefferson. Then, two years later, in June 2002, I was invited to be one of the presenters at the UVA symposium entitled "Writing the Life of Thomas Jefferson." This symposium gave me the opportunity to articulate my reasons for writing the new book and my goals for it. The opportunity to read sections of it aloud to Jefferson scholars and hear their reactions to it was invaluable.

Most significant – and delightful – was getting to know Annette Gordon-Reed, who was at that time researching and writing what would become her brilliant Pulitzer Prize winning book, *The Hemingses of Monticello*. She made a profound impact on my thinking about Jefferson and slavery, and responded fully to my queries concerning my manuscript. She gave me the courage to pursue this topic. Ultimately, I was privileged to call her my friend. Her daughter, Susan Reed, shared with me her unique perspective on my telling of Jefferson's story and made some fine suggestions.

Great people inspire others to search for the greatness within themselves. We all need heroes to inspire us. But what constitutes a hero? Must one be considered perfect in **every** respect before being considered a hero? Might a flawed human being be a hero?

The Greek philosopher Plato conceived of the human soul as perpetually drawn by two horses, one white and the other black, one pulling the soul up toward the highest in its nature, the other dragging it down to the lowest. A successful biographer is one who can see both and can show how someone who has this difficult pair to drive can succeed as well as fail. Indeed, it is the negotiation within a person – between strength and weakness – that ultimately determines the hero. An ordinary person *can* become a hero.

Thomas Jefferson seems a perfect example of this concept, and it is a theme that I explore in the second book.

I have placed Jefferson in the context of slavery, on his mountaintop and in his world. This was my attempt to bring to life a man who was born into a society in which slavery was ubiquitous and to show how the institution of slavery resonated throughout his life. By 1775 nearly half the population in Virginia were slaves, and slavery had become essential to plantation economy. Thus, the climate of opinion of the times must become the foundation on which Jefferson's story rests.

I have tried to examine the issue of slavery in general, as well as to provide an in-depth look at slave life at Monticello. I hope my readers will see Monticello as a real place – a working plantation – and they will see Jefferson's world as he saw it, and to the extent that it is possible, as his slaves saw it.

Thomas Jefferson's often contradictory ideas and actions on slavery and race relations are causing much concern about how to judge him. Personally, I find that more than twenty-eight years after my first biography of Thomas Jefferson was published and more than nine years after my second book, Thomas Jefferson continues to intrigue me. I am still addressing these questions and attempting to enrich my understanding of the man.

I read all the new material being published about him and slavery. It is a compelling topic that seems to have no end. New information continues to come to light, and I am always eager to read it. I was particularly interested in the portrayal of Jefferson in the Broadway hit musical "Hamilton" that opened during the summer of 2015. A biographer's interest in her subject never diminishes. Indeed, at present I am preparing a talk that will explore the opposing views of Thomas Jefferson and Alexander Hamilton as they relate to the formative years of our nation.

Jefferson's most enduring legacy has been a particular understanding of personal freedom – a philosophy of fundamental human rights as he expressed it in the Declaration of Independence and in his Statute of Virginia for Religious Freedom:

His passion for civil liberties and his belief in what he described as "the illimitable freedom of the human mind" radiates through his extraordinary *Bill for Establishing Religious Freedom* (1779), his most profound state paper. Here Jefferson drafted what he considered the "fulfillment of the philosophy of the Declaration of Independence." It is an eloquent manifesto of the sanctity of the human mind, arguing not only for religious freedom (separation of church and state), but for intellectual liberty as well. We cannot measure Jefferson's greatness without considering this!

And, it is his incandescent writing in the Declaration of Independence that gives us his sharpest self-portrait.

But reference to the Declaration invariably brings up the question of how its author could have written such ringing words about equality and freedom, yet remain a slaveholder. That his life was a paradox is notorious. But can we – indeed dare we – ignore the words that flowed from what John Adams called his "masterly pen" expressing the most potent idea of modern history, that all men are created equal?

The most important thing to remember about Thomas Jefferson is that he taught us the power of the word. He taught us that ideas matter – that words beautifully shaped can reshape lives. Indeed, in the words he wrote he changed the shape of our country and became one of the most notable champions of freedom and enlightenment in recorded history. He had a vision of what the world *should* be. Even before his death, the language of the Declaration was appropriated by new claimants – freed Blacks, abolitionists, early advocates of women's rights – until it received decisive transformation by Abraham Lincoln at Gettysburg, when he said: "We are a nation dedicated to the proposition that all men are created equal." Thomas Jefferson wrote that proposition.

History is an argument without end. That is its fascination. We will never all agree on Jefferson, but the recent focus on race and slavery has enriched our understanding of him. While we have not validated one or another opinion on Jefferson, we know more now than we ever knew. But much of it does not have to do with Sally Hemings. It is not the question of a possible sexual relationship that is important in itself. As historian John Hope Franklin said so eloquently, "The fact that he owned her is."

We must situate Jefferson in a series of horizons –on his mountaintop plantation, as a Virginian, as a nationalist, and as a man of the entire world – a man of the Enlightenment – a man of his time. We must consider carefully what it meant to be a man of his time.

As a wife, mother, grandmother, and great-grandmother working on one biography after another, I often dreamed of having an opportunity to go someplace where I could research, think, and write without interruption. So imagine my supreme delight when I received a letter inviting me to become a fellow at the International Center for Jefferson Studies! Dreams *can* come true.

What I was being offered, in addition to a small allowance, was the opportunity to live, for two months at a time, in a charming little cottage just steps away from the Thomas Jefferson Presidential Library (the only presidential library dedicated to a founding father), and approximately half a mile from Monticello and all that it has to offer. I was off on another treasure hunt.

How fortunate I was to have access to the superb resources of the Jefferson Library! I can't imagine any other place where I could have made as much progress on my work. I had my own office in the library, with ample shelves for my own books. Ceiling to floor windows allowed the light to flood the room and gave me a view of the magnificent foliage just outside. The research librarian was just down the hall, ready to answer any questions I might have, and to locate for me just the right book and/or archival material that I needed. In addition, there were Jefferson scholars working in the library who were always happy to discuss Mr. Jefferson with me from their varied perspectives. They brought my research to a higher level of scholarship. Having them nearby helped sharpen my focus, enrich my understanding, and move my writing forward.

The author at work in her office in the Jefferson Library
Photo courtesy of L.H. Bober

Exploring the mountaintop for a second time was yet another enlightening experience. Touring Monticello, Jefferson's unique laboratory, was an eye-opener. I was able to sit in a chair placed at a window, where I could understand why Jefferson insisted on floor to ceiling windows at a time when glass had to be imported from England and was, therefore, very expensive. Indeed, when the only light after the sun went down was derived from candles, the tall windows allowed much more light to enter the rooms than did ordinary windows. Thus, Jefferson could read for longer periods of time. Being there – and getting to know Susan Stein, curator of Monticello - made it possible for me to "read" Monticello as a work of art, with Thomas Jefferson as the artist.

I was taken up to the dome room, a large circular room (about twenty-six feet in diameter) with eight circular windows and a beautiful skylight. Constructed in 1800, and modeled after the Temple of Vesta in Rome, it is the first dome on a house in America. Jefferson had first seen a dome on the Hals Aux Bleds, a large, noisy grain market in Paris, when he was living there as Minister to the French Court in 1785. Its giant dome captured his imagination, as it did mine when I saw it on my first visit to Paris. It would appear later on Monticello. Jefferson sometimes called the dome room his sky room. What a delightful space it must have been for his grandchildren to play in.

I viewed the house and the grounds, the vegetable gardens and the flowers, as Bill Beiswanger, Architectural Historian, and Peter Hatch, Director of Gardens & Grounds, brought into sharper focus the relationship between Jefferson's development and the development of Monticello. Seeing the house and gardens a second time through their eyes brought to life the "human" Jefferson.

I walked along Mulberry Row, the thousand-foot-long road just south of the main house, named by Jefferson after the mulberry trees that lined it. Mulberry Row was the home of the slave quarters and the hub of all the activities that the laboring community engaged in: Jefferson's slaves were cabinet-makers, carpenters, masons, bricklayers, and blacksmiths, among other trades.

The South Pavilion, or "Honeymoon Cottage" (as it

was sometimes called), clinging to the side of a steep slope, was the first structure erected at Monticello, and the one to which Jefferson took his new bride, Martha. They traveled through three feet of snow on horseback because the snow was too deep for their phaeton (a two-horse carriage) to navigate. I was taken inside this tiny building to see the one room that served as living room, dining room, and bedroom. The kitchen was in the basement, one floor below.

Perhaps the most significant aspect of my fellowship at ICJS and my extended stay there was the opportunity to expand my understanding of black oral history. Lucia (Cinder) Stanton, Shannon Senior Historian at Monticello, was always happy to spend time with me, describing "Getting Word," her black oral history project. She began her groundbreaking research and writing on Monticello's slaves in 1993 in order to preserve the histories of the African American families at Jefferson's Monticello. Two of her books, *Slavery at Monticello* and *Those Who Labor for My Happiness*, were indispensable. They do justice to both Jefferson and his slaves.

My husband and I stayed in the "Roosevelt Cottage." Just a bit larger than the South Pavilion, it was built and named for President Franklin Delano Roosevelt. The president slept there for just one night. Often, when we awoke in the morning, we would find two deer eating the apples from the trees in front of the house or simply peering in the living-room window.

Roosevelt Cottage
Photo courtesy of L.H. Bober

To walk just the few steps between the library and the cottage at noon, to share lunch with my husband as well as share with him some of what I had learned and/ or written that morning, then return to work refreshed, was a joy. Later, at the close of the working day, we had wine and cheese on the terrace, in the shade of those old apple trees, before driving off to one of the fine restaurants in the area. This was the icing on the cake.

Author's Note / Summing Up

Research *can* be exciting, for me perhaps more so even than the writing, because when I'm researching I'm learning. It's like a game, a treasure hunt. I'm playing detective, and the excitement comes from search and discovery – from recreating a life from details.

As you have seen, research takes many forms: reading books, periodicals, all kinds of printed material, old newspapers (e.g. *Old Virginia Gazette*); sifting through archives; and seeing your subject's handwriting in letters. Sitting in the American Antiquarian Society in Worcester, Massachusetts, reading Adams's letters to her sister Mary had a huge impact on me. I could sense the love that existed between them, and the dependence Abigail always felt on this beloved older sister. I felt so close to her that I could almost hear her voice!

Reading Louise Nevelson's letters to and from her young son who was living with his aunt in Rockland,

Maine, while his mother was in Germany studying art with Hans Hoffman, gave me an insight into their relationship that I could not have acquired anywhere else. Indeed, you have seen how Abigail Adams's letters were her autobiography, and how they showed us the human side of the American Revolution.

We must hear the voices of the past before we can write about it.

Also important are diaries, journals, account books, bills, and plans such as Jefferson's drawings of Monticello. Equally essential are conducting interviews, attending conferences and lectures, and studying paintings and photographs.

Perhaps most important, I read everything. I turn every page. But this is one place where being a rapid reader is not an asset. Haste is the enemy of scholarship. It's the thinking that takes time. You must have some notion of why you are copying a particular fact or incident. What will it do for a scene or a chapter? What does it reveal about your subject? Will it move your story forward?

Sometimes these choices are very hard to make. Hours of reading may offer up only one or two sentences to convey the feeling, the flavor of the times or the person. But I have learned that it is this selection that determines the ultimate product.

Conducting interviews can also be an important tool. But here, we must know the right questions to ask, and the right people to question. We must first do our homework. We must have some sense of what it is we need to know that we can't learn anywhere else. And – we must listen carefully to the answers. If possible, I try to turn an interview into a conversation, rather than a list of questions.

But documents and interviews can never tell it all. I have to go to the territory. Being in an area where a scene or an event I'm describing took place, among landscapes and buildings that my characters knew, lends a sense of place. It makes it possible for me to know the effect that place had on my subject. Travel, then, becomes an essential part of research for me. It helps me to learn more about people and places, and to feel almost a part of my subject's life.

I could never have written about Thomas Jefferson's Monticello had I not seen it myself. Pictures alone could never tell the story. And only when I visited Williamsburg, Virginia, and walked the streets of this city of living history, was I able to visualize the young Thomas Jefferson living there when he was a student at the College of William and Mary. It gave me some sense of the richness and complexity of the times in which he lived. For me, the language of landscape is crucial to understanding my subject.

The purpose of writing is to think and to learn. My drafts become a lens, helping me to see my subject from a new perspective. I use language as a tool for seeing and understanding. We do not write **what** we know so much as we write **to** know. Writing then, becomes exploration. We must be curious: we must listen; we must be observant; we must ask a lot of questions. The joy is in how we examine the evidence, how we construct theories, how we explain perplexing situations. We must look for new connections. There must be connections between our lives and what we are learning in our research. Most importantly, the good biographer combines the detective work of the historian, the insight of the psychologist, and the art of the novelist.

I'm often asked, "How do you choose your subjects?" This must be done very carefully. The biographer is going to live with a subject for a very long time, so there must be an affinity. As I look back over the lives I have portrayed, I realize that they all had much in common.

They were all rebels – gentle rebels, to be sure, but rebels nonetheless. All had the same approach to learning: they lost themselves in books or in their art when they were young, all found power in knowledge and believed in the freedom of the human mind. All had a quiet determination, a faith in themselves, and a strong belief in the freedom of their materials.

A biographer may spend four to five years (and often longer) with a subject. In reading what truly great people said and wrote, in learning about them as they erred, stumbled, fell and rose again, and in watching their wisdom and their talent develop, a biographer cannot help but be impacted by their lives. She will never be the same again.

In my own case, I really believe my subjects chose me. And I think that many biographers will tell you the same thing.

I came to William Wordsworth and then Robert Frost through my love of their poetry. For me, Robert Frost's story was a natural sequence to William Wordsworth's: I think of Frost as the American Wordsworth. As I said earlier, both wrote in "language really used by man." There was no question in my mind that he would be my next subject.

Louise Nevelson's wooden assemblages spoke to me from the first time I saw one. Both she and Marc Chagall called to me with their unique way of seeing. Thomas Jefferson had been a hero of mine since my childhood. In the words he wrote he changed the shape of our country and became one of the most notable champions of freedom and enlightenment in recorded history. Abigail Adams jumped out to me as an extraordinary woman when first I "met" her as I wrote about Thomas Jefferson. She spoke out for equal rights for women, particularly their right to an education and their right to vote. She was, truly, witness to a revolution, and she showed us, by her example, the value of letter writing.

As I think back now on all the books I have written, I become more and more aware of how each one is, in some sense, a part of my autobiography. I often find myself describing a particular time or an event in my life according to which biography I was writing at the time, just as my grandmother defined her life in terms of the dates of birth of her six children.

Always, as I write, I have in mind something written by Sir Sidney Lee (1859-1926), editor of the Dictionary of National Biography in England, and known for his biography of William Shakespeare. He wrote: "The aim of biography is the truthful transmission of personality."

A good biographer is under oath to interpret the material she has gathered honestly. As I write, I try to recreate as truthfully yet as powerfully as I can, the world that is unfolding before me, for if I paint a picture colored by my priorities, it is a false one.

I remember, too, a statement by the French writer and critic Anatole France who said, "Do not try to satisfy your vanity by teaching a great many things. Awaken people's curiosity. It is enough to open minds; do not overload them. Put there just a spark. If there is some inflammable stuff, it will catch fire."

As I write this I am excited by the thought that I recently had my first picture book for young children published! Because of an eye problem, I am no longer able to do the kind of research I used to do for my biographies. It occurred to me that I might use one of the subjects about whom I had already written, and find a story that would lend itself to a picture book format. Not knowing whether or not I could write in the proper voice, but loving the challenge, I decided to try. I wrote it and the first editor who read it accepted it – a far cry from the twenty-one rejections that my first book had garnered! It is called *Papa Is A Poet,* and is a story about the poet Robert Frost, told from the perspective of his young daughter Lesley. It was illustrated by an artist in England, Rebecca Gibbon, and was published in 2013.

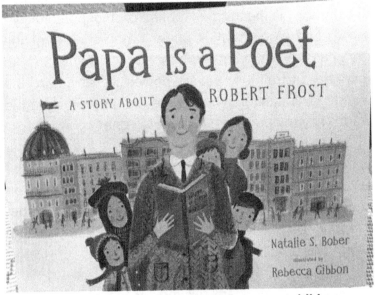

The author's first picture book for young children
Photo courtesy of Rebecca Gibbon

As I muse on this happening, I am struck by the fact that, once again, as I did with my first biography, I have turned a physical handicap into a new genre of writing for me, and a prize-winning book. Perhaps I am off on a new adventure!

CPSIA information can be obtained
at www.ICGtesting.com
Printed in the USA
BVOW08s0809300417
482660BV00001B/37/P